BUCKINGHA
TALES OF M
AND MURDER

Other titles in this series include:

BUCKINGHAMSHIRE TALES OF MYSTERY AND MURDER

David Kidd-Hewitt

COUNTRYSIDE BOOKS
NEWBURY, BERKSHIRE

First published 2003
© David Kidd-Hewitt 2003

COUNTRYSIDE BOOKS
3 Catherine Road
Newbury, Berkshire

To view our complete range of books,
please visit us at
www.countrysidebooks.co.uk

ISBN 1 85306 809 8

Designed by Mon Mohan

Produced through MRM Associates Ltd., Reading
Typeset by Mac Style Ltd, Scarborough, N. Yorkshire
Printed by J.W. Arrowsmith Ltd., Bristol

Contents

MAP OF BUCKINGHAMSHIRE

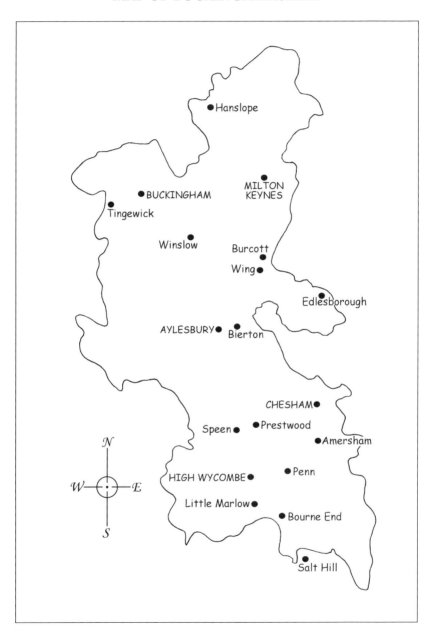

This book is especially for Jan, Rachel and Paul
and to the memory of Shelley

ACKNOWLEDGEMENTS

————————❖————————

Researching these Buckinghamshire tales has been an interesting and absorbing journey and all the more rewarding because of the leads and information supplied by those I have met on the way.

Grateful thanks to the Centre for Buckinghamshire Studies and to Bill Torrens for leading me to Alice Turney. Thank you Alison Heath, Archivist at Wycombe Abbey School, for such kind hospitality and invaluable assistance.

I also want to record my thanks to Frances, Val and Penny at Great Missenden Library for their help in obtaining reference material essential to my research. To all those who told me their stories and let me into their homes, Noel and Louise, Brian and Christine, John and Jacolyn, Angus and Aila, I am very grateful and hope you like the results. Thanks also to Steve Cohen, editor of the *Bucks Free Press*, and to the British Library for permission to reproduce the *Bucks Free Press* front page, headlining the murder of David Blakely by Ruth Ellis.

To Janet Bord for kindly allowing me to include her Tingewick 'ghost dog' photograph and to Ron Unwin for the use of Bill Corkett's photograph.

Finally, heartfelt thanks to Jan for her continued support even through my Victor Meldrew times.

THE HAUNTED VINEGAR BOWL

❖
————————————

'A man suddenly in Shoolane' 10th July 1665

This anonymous man dying 'suddenly' in London's Shoe Lane has the dubious distinction of being the first recorded victim of the infamous Great Plague of 1665.

When the fast-spreading disease hit London that scorching summer with around 100 deaths every three to four days, those who could afford to do so, fled the city for the countryside. Protecting oneself from this invisible horror became a fixation. London's watermen took their wives and families in their wherries as far as possible upstream. Tradesmen who valued their life more than their money locked up their premises, posted a hasty sign, *'Closed at the Behest of the Dreaded Plague'*, and fled.

Those forced to stay in the affected areas would struggle to maintain bonfires night and day in the belief that only the power of fire could swallow the stench and eat this evil pestilence knocking at their door.

The pleasant green countryside of Buckinghamshire was seen as a safe haven by many who could afford to rent or buy a cottage, thereby isolating themselves from the contamination. Indeed, the village of Chalfont St Giles became home to the famous poet John Milton (1608–1674) who fled Bunhill Fields in London in fear of his life. The plague had no more respect for writers and poets than for any other human being.

Although people were safer in rural Buckinghamshire, they could still be touched by the plague and the destruction of life continued, albeit not as rapidly as in the crowded city. Slowly but surely, the disease reached out its putrefying hand and claimed victim after victim. Plague pits became a common feature, each county burying its dead in designated areas, where the bodies were slaked with lime to speed the process of rotting and disintegration.

As fire, lime and country air were not enough to halt the plague's steady progress, so grew the practice of using vinegar bowls.

Outside your farm or cottage you would arrange a stone bowl or sometimes a small trough filled with vinegar. All the money that you owed a local tradesman would be placed in this receptacle so it could be taken away, hopefully cleansed of the plague, and any change would be left there for you to collect.

At this time, in the Buckinghamshire village of Priestwood (now Prestwood), in a long lost lane called Back Lane, was sited one cottage and two farms, Greenlands Farm and Hampden Farm.

The cottage is no longer there but a farm building remains to this day in what is now known as Greenlands Lane. Also to be seen, close to Hampden Farm, set in an old flint stone wall, is an original plague vinegar bowl.

The wall is near the old footpath that would have led you straight to the small thatched cottage, but the vinegar bowl itself is very easy to miss. It retired many centuries ago from performing its battle with the plague virus and is now overgrown with ivy. But if you take the time to part the leaves carefully, you can, if you concentrate, just make out what appears to be a worn, leering face carved in stone at the back of the bowl.

Not everyone, it must be confessed, can see it, however long they stare. But be warned, whatever you do, do not place your hand into its shallow well for this vinegar bowl is said to be haunted.

Long after the plague had been swept away and the vinegar had dried to a dark crimson stain, it still came in useful for leaving the milkman a note and his weekly milk money. So its life continued, hands going in and out of its indentation, exchanging money and messages.

One stormy morning, so the story goes, in 1865, 200 years after the outbreak of the plague, the local horse-drawn milk cart clattered its way down the muddy track to the cottage footpath. Bill Cherry, a cheerful man whatever the weather, whistled as he reined in his horse alongside the bowl. Admittedly the facts are a little confusing about the events that followed, but there is no doubt, as the weather records tell us, that a fierce, freak thunderstorm broke out across the morning sky. Ferocious jagged lightning cast an eerie glow across a still visible moon, its fingers pointing out a destructive path, breaking boughs and crackling threateningly around the thatched roofs and stable yards. Bill's horse started, but his calming voice told her to '... hold steady girl, we'll soon be away and warm'.

Still whistling, Bill clambered down from his small cab, grabbed the dispensing churn and ladle from the back and, as if impervious to the lashing rain, measured out his milk delivery into the waiting cottage urn.

Craaaaaaaaaaaaaaack, the lightning continued in its fury.

Bill quickly placed the churn back on board and automatically reached into the vinegar bowl for his money.

At that moment, a bolt of lightning shot its jagged arm towards the very same spot. It lit up a leering, evil face carved on the inside stone of the bowl. Bill had never even noticed this before and he felt uneasy. His horse reared up terrified and as he glanced quickly away to calm her, he felt his hand being grabbed and squeezed as if in a vice. Crying out in pain, he tried to pull away from the vinegar bowl, but to no avail. A second flash of lightning then revealed the horror he was never to forget.

A withering, festering, putrid hand, as if from a corpse, was clasped around his in a bizarre handshake. His own hand was slowly but surely being pulled down into the bowl, his fingers crushed and in agony.

Then, as suddenly as it began, his hand was freed. He screamed in relief and bewilderment, leaping onto his cart and shouting, 'In God's name go girl, GO, for God's sake, GO.' The terrified horse needed no encouragement and flew, the milk churns falling and rolling from the cart as they escaped. Bill's mind was in a turmoil.

It was true that later that morning when the storm had cleared, several of Bill's churns were found strewn about the lane. It was also true that he had neglected to collect his money from the bowl that morning. But even more strange was the addition of two freshly minted farthing coins lying amongst the milk money. They both bore the date 1665.

No one could explain how they got there.

It was also true that from that day onwards, after a terrified Bill had told his tale, his mental state deteriorated so he was no longer able to work. He took to sitting in his cottage mumbling, the

The milkman on his way home from Winslow, c.1925 – a scene little changed since Bill Cherry delivered his milk by horse and cart in 1865. (© Wolverton & District Archaeological Society)

fingers on his right hand weeping raw stumps. This was not from any disease as far as anyone could tell, but hour after hour, day after day and year after year, Bill tried every means to scrub them clean from the putrid stench that was always with him. He was literally rubbing his fingers away. The strange thing was that no one else could smell it, but Bill took no heed and it always seemed to him to be much worse in the summer, especially in July.

July 10th to be exact, Bill's birthday.

Bill hadn't always lived in the country, in fact he was born in East London.

In Shoe Lane to be precise.

THE PETIT BEURRE
MYSTERY

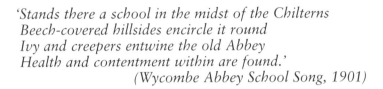

'Stands there a school in the midst of the Chilterns
Beech-covered hillsides encircle it round
Ivy and creepers entwine the old Abbey
Health and contentment within are found.'
(Wycombe Abbey School Song, 1901)

The icy waters closed over the girls' heads as they screamed and thrashed about. Desperately they struggled to survive but the powerful winter currents had other plans. Cries of anguish, terror and pain wrought the air, 'Please help us, don't let us drown.'

The young schoolmistress woke with a start. She sat alone in her sparsely furnished room, trembling with shock at the scene she had just witnessed. It was a recurring nightmare so real that she had to do something about it. However, she had not worked at Wycombe Abbey School very long, and she did not want the headmistress to think she was strange or unstable.

Whenever these vivid dreams occurred, all she could do was to remain awake. She would sit in bed for the rest of the night, sipping tea and munching her favourite petit beurre biscuits to take her mind off that terrible vision. The girls in her nightmare tragedy were clearly from the school. There was no mistaking their distinctive dark blue uniforms. She even recognised some of their faces, or thought she did.

They seemed to blur into one special girl whose eyes, filled with fear, would look directly at her, pleading for help as the water closed over her head.

Eventually this dream became a torment that she carried round with her day after day. Was it a warning, she wondered, a premonition perhaps? Before long she plucked up courage to speak to Miss Dove, the headmistress, about her experience and the terrible worry she felt. Miss Dove was sympathetic, if a little concerned about the mental anguish this young teacher was suffering. She always put the girls first and her staff were expected to sacrifice everything to ensure that the welfare of the pupils was paramount. No one could give of their best while coping with sleepless nights and such anxiety. However, the teacher felt better having shared her burden and the dreams did begin to fade and then stop altogether.

Unbeknown to that young teacher, Miss Dove herself had experienced dreams that also saw her girls in the fast flowing waters of the River Thames. But, in Miss Dove's dream, the girls were not in difficulties; on the contrary, they were accomplished rowers. She had dreamt she was standing on Marlow Bridge when she noticed an eight-oar boat coming towards her. She too recognised the Wycombe Abbey School colours, and, again, was able to make out the faces of individual girls.

All this had left Miss Dove with one important thought. If her dream could come true, as she hoped, so could the terrible tragedy witnessed by the young teacher. She had already considered instituting swimming lessons as part of the school's activities, but now they were essential. There was to be no boating on the nearby River Thames until all the girls had learnt to swim.

The school prided itself on producing the finest educated young ladies possible, but with much more than just academic talents. Miss Dove believed strongly in the fostering of athletic skills in girls, curtly dismissing any claim that such activities were only male prerogatives. In a remarkable statement for its time and only two years after her pioneering work in the founding of the school in 1896, Miss Dove had written in an essay entitled *The Cultivation of the Body*, 'We do not desire girls to be brainless athletes any more than we wish that they should be delicate or stunted blue-stockings.'

Right from its late 19th century beginnings, Wycombe Abbey had become a much sought after public school for girls. The enterprising and far-seeing Miss Dove, true to her principles that girls were at least equal to, if not better than, boys, based her school on the male public school model and then took it that much further in terms of the 'Health and Contentment' so heartily sung about in the school song of 1901.

She also allowed a great deal of fun to be had at the school: 'Let us have games of all kinds, lawn tennis, fives, bowls, croquet, quoits, golf, swimming, skating, archery, tobogganing, basketball, rounders and hailes,' she wrote. For Miss Dove there was 'no finer exercise than swimming'. That and her passion for Swedish Gymnastics, that claimed to provide systematic training of all the body's muscles.

True to progressing her dream, Miss Dove had, by 1904, encouraged the formation of a 'boat committee' which took every advantage of the magnificent school lake. A few pupils even took to the water of the Thames in July 1904 under the scornful gaze and sarcastic comments of the ferrymen at Townsend's Wharf at Bourne End. When, led by another young teacher, Miss Batchelor, the girls asked for two poles and two paddles, one boatman said in a scathing tone, 'Oh, you be going to do some work, you be?' and the men all laughed.

It was, however, on another visit to that same wharf in Bourne End a few years later that our main story unfolds.

It was a crisp, frosty Saturday on 2nd February 1907. The girls awoke earlier than usual just to be sure that the weather hadn't changed. Squeals of excitement told that it had not. The school

Looking across the River Thames at Cockmarsh – scene of the boating incident

grounds were covered in a heavy white frost and the lake was frozen solid.

Today, they were going skating.

Skating on the school lake, however, was much too dangerous and strictly forbidden by Miss Dove. But this didn't matter because their trip was to be much more exciting. The whole school of 200 girls was going to a popular skating area in Bourne End called Cockmarsh.

This damp, boggy piece of land was transformed in frosty winter weather into a magnificent natural skating rink, totally safe and fantastic fun.

After a swift but nutritious breakfast – Miss Dove had very specific views on the value of porridge to start the day – they set off to catch the 8.28 am train from High Wycombe to Bourne End. All of them were under strict instructions to represent the very best image of the school.

With their skates tied around their necks, they clutched their packed lunches, lots of chocolate and other goodies to ward off the cold. This was going to be a great day out. There was plenty of excited chattering and giggling about the great time they were about to have and the boys that they might bump into – literally.

The train chugged through the frosty winter morning, steam billowing across the frozen landscape and in a matter of 20 minutes they were alighting at Bourne End Station. Already, people were arriving from all directions to enjoy a Saturday on the ice. To reach Cockmarsh, however, there was another exciting adventure to experience. A ferry ride across the Thames. The river's flow was too fast to allow it to become frozen enough to walk on so this was the only way to reach the skating meadow on the opposite bank.

Ferries were already busy plying their trade from Townsend's Wharf across to Cockmarsh and soon it was the turn of the Wycombe Abbey girls to cross. They split into groups and the first set off to arrive moments later on the Cockmarsh side of the river.

The second party got ready to join them but what happened next was totally unexpected and very dangerous. The subsequent newspaper stories also differ slightly in their accounts of the events that were to follow, as did the account given by the girls themselves to their school magazine. For us, it is important that we have three, independently published, accounts of the events that morning.

According to an eyewitness for the *South Bucks Standard*, the ferry-punt had soon filled up with excited girls anxious to join their companions already on the other side, who were busy putting on their skates. The ferryman swung the punt around so that the bow faced the opposite bank and had just set off when, in the words of the reported eyewitness, '... two or three impetuous spirits thought they might fill up a small vacant place and so they jumped for it.'

The girls would, in their later report, blame the ferryman for overloading the boat, but it does seem that some over-enthusiastic skaters did leap into the boat after it had begun the journey across.

Immediately this happened, the stern was forced below the fast flowing, freezing cold water of the Thames. It rushed into the punt, swamping the occupants and tipping around thirty of them into the icy cold river. All was panic and confusion and screams for help.

Wycombe Abbey girls break for lunch at Cockmarsh, Bourne End, in 1919, several years after the ferry adventure. (© Wycombe Abbey School)

Some of the young women had been thrown into deeper waters than others, whilst those who could scrambled out, pulled by willing hands. Those in deeper water were forced to brave the shock of their sudden cold immersion and swim to the bank. Some girls were certainly out of their depth and screaming with shock but, encouraged by shouts from those on the bank, made it to their eager helpers who pulled them shivering from the river. The later report in the school magazine spoke of how they '... instinctively struck out and began to swim'.

When it became clear that all had survived, it seemed that Miss Dove's insistence on learning swimming skills had paid off. One group of shivering girls was rushed to the nearby Ferry Hotel, where the landlady, Mrs Cleve, wrapped them in blankets beside the pub fire. The other group hurried to the Railway Hotel and were also made warm and comfortable. Messages were sent to Wycombe Abbey School for dry clothing to be dispatched as quickly as possible and a mixture of all sorts of cosy, warm clothes eventually arrived at both hotels.

The Railway Hotel at Bourne End where some of the girls were taken to recover from their ordeal. (Reproduced by kind permission of the Bourne End Residents' Association)

All subsequent reports of the incident agree that the girls were very brave and in remarkably high spirits given the nature of their ordeal. They were much sadder, however, when they saw their friends who had made the ferry trip safely returning from their skating fun, but in their own way they knew they had experienced a remarkable adventure and a fortunate escape.

However, whilst the *South Bucks Free Press*, the following Friday, played down the danger and reported 'An Exciting Incident and Amusing Adventure', the eyewitness reporter for the *South Bucks Standard* provided a more realistic assessment. Under the headline 'Startling Accident near the Ferry: Young Ladies Immersed', it took a far more serious line. Taking into account that there was an exceptionally heavy frost that day and the girls had been tipped suddenly into icy water wearing heavy coats, boots, scarves and gloves, carrying skates and packed lunches, then under some circumstances this might have ended more tragically. What the *South Bucks Standard* referred to as the possibility of '... a fatal termination'.

The report paid tribute to '... the brave and healthy outlook on life and its happenings which their school precepts induce them to hold'.

After congratulating the victims on their escape and plucky behaviour, certain others at Wycome Abbey got to thinking about the young teacher who had now left the school and how she awoke startled on so many occasions with her terrible dream until she had the courage to mention her fears to the headmistress. We do not know if, secretly, Miss Dove paid silent homage to that teacher's second sight which had led her to issue the all important directive that, without exception, every one of her girls must learn to swim.

There is, however, one more intriguing part to this story – a piece of information that does not appear in the newspaper reports about the Bourne End ferry incident. A piece of information that, at first glance, seems relatively trivial and can be found only in the school's own termly journal *The Gazette* of June 1907. Recalling what happened on the morning of 2nd February under the heading 'Skating Holiday', it records the accident very much as the newspapers had except they blamed the ferryman for allowing too many to board and then pushing off from the bank too suddenly. Whoever was to blame, however, makes no difference to what follows in the *The Gazette's* report. Apart from the hats, gloves, scarves and other items of clothing that were left floating in the river, the magazine records: 'There were innumerable "Petit Beurre" biscuits, which had been bought for lunch, in the water, and when the other lost articles were collected and sent back to Wycombe, some industrious individual carefully gathered together all the scraps of biscuit and returned them as well. They have since been very much enjoyed by the swans on the lake.'

Who on earth would bother to do such a thing as collect scraps of broken, soggy petit beurre biscuits from an icy, fast-flowing river and take the trouble to return them, anonymously but neatly wrapped, to the school? Was this a final mysterious sign that those endless nightmare nights endured by the young teacher had achieved their purpose?

Second sight is a rare gift indeed. It was now up to Miss Dove to realise her dream.

THE FINAL RESTING PLACE OF RUTH ELLIS

❖

'The fact stands out like a beacon that this young man became an absolute necessity to this young woman. However brutally he behaved, and however much he spent of her money on various entertainments of his own, and however much he consorted with other people, he ultimately came back to her, and she always forgave him. She found herself in something like an emotional prison guarded by this young man from which there seemed to be no escape.'

(Melford Stevenson, QC, Defence Lawyer for Ruth Ellis)

In life, their relationship was tempestuous and violent. It ended in one of the most famous murder trials of the 20th century. It also ended with a hanging that to this day continues to be challenged as unjust.

Now in death, they lie in different Buckinghamshire churchyards, one in an unmarked grave in Amersham, the other buried in Penn, the victim of a cold-blooded murder. But is it all as it seems?

Is there a murderer buried in Amersham and an innocent victim buried in Penn?

In the unmarked grave lies Ruth Ellis, who has taken on the infamous role of the last woman to be executed in Britain. She was a mother of two small children who had suffered a recent miscarriage after being punched in the stomach by her lover from Penn, David Blakely.

She shot him five times on 10th April 1955, an Easter Sunday afternoon, in Hampstead.

Ever since this landmark murder trial, the debate has raged about whether justice was done when Ruth Ellis was hanged on 13th July 1955 at Holloway Prison. Her cause of death, as posted to the silent crowds who gathered outside was 'Injuries to the central nervous system consequent upon judicial hanging'.

There is no dispute that Ruth Ellis shot David Blakely with intent to kill and that the last of her five shots was fired at point-blank range as he lay wounded on the ground outside the Magdala public house in South Hill Park, Hampstead. Indeed, at her trial, when the prosecuting counsel Mr Christmas Humphries asked Ruth, 'Miss Ellis, when you fired that revolver at close range into the body of David Blakely, what did you intend to do?', her reply was unambiguous, 'It was obvious that when I shot him, I intended to kill him.'

So why do so many people see a victim rather than a murderer now lying in that unmarked Amersham grave? Indeed, why is Ruth Ellis in Amersham at all when her colourful nightclub life had no connections with what she would regard as a boring Buckinghamshire village? She was a glamorous club manageress in Kensington, not a village girl.

Ruth was born in Wales, in Rhyl, in 1926 and had no connections with Amersham whatsoever. Also, as an executed murderess, she had been buried in unconsecrated ground within the walls of Holloway Prison, not a village churchyard in the Buckinghamshire countryside. To fully understand her crime and the location and significance of her final resting place, we need to explore the true emotions and tensions that characterised Ruth and David's relationship.

Perhaps one of the clearest statements of Ruth's feelings is contained in a letter she wrote to David Blakely's mother, a few days after she had murdered him. Written on prison notepaper from Holloway on Tuesday 12th April it arrived at 'The Old Park', Hammersley Lane in Penn, received by a grieving mother and family yet to bury their son at Penn parish church.

Providing some of the emotional clues that take us closer to the reasons why both Ruth and David could, in many ways, be seen as victims and are now living closer to each other in death than in life, the letter is addressed simply to Mrs Cook. *(David's mother had remarried in 1941 and David's stepfather was Humphrey Wyndham Cook. Ruth's letter is reproduced exactly as written by prisoner 9656, HM Prison, Holloway, London N7, spelling mistakes included.)*

DEAR MRS COOK,
NO DOUGHT THESE LAST FEW DAYS HAVE BEEN A SHOCK TO YOU.

PLEASE TRY TO BELIEVE ME, WHEN I SAY, HOW DEEPLY SORRY
I AM TO HAVE CAUSED YOU THIS UNPLEASANTNESS.

NO DOUGHT YOU WILL KNOW ALL KINDS OF STORIES REGARDING DAVID AND I. PLEASE DO FORGIVE HIM FOR DECIEVING YOU, HAS REGARDING MYSELF.

DAVID AND I HAVE SPENT MANY HAPPY TIMES TOGETHER. THURSDAY 7TH APRIL, DAVID ARRIVED HOME AT 7.15 PM HE GAVE ME THE LATEST PHOTOGRAPH HE HAD, A FEW DAYS HENCE HAD TAKEN, HE TOLD ME HE HAD GIVEN YOU ONE.

FRIDAY MORNING AT 10 O'CLOCK HE LEFT AND PROMISED TO RETURN AT 8 O'CLOCK BUT NEVER DID. THE TWO PEOPLE I BLAME FOR DAVID'S DEATH, AND MY OWN, ARE THE FINLAYTERS. NO DOUGHT YOU WILL NOT UNDERSTAND THIS BUT PERHAPS BEFORE I HANG YOU WILL KNOW WHAT I MEAN.

PLEASE EXCUSE MY WRITING, BUT THE PEN IS SHOCKING.

I IMPLORE YOU TO TRY AND FORGIVE DAVID FOR LIVING WITH ME, BUT WE WERE VERY MUCH IN LOVE WITH ONE ANOTHER UNFORTUNATELY DAVID WAS NOT SATISFIED WITH ONE WOMAN IN HIS LIFE.

I HAVE FORGIVEN DAVID, I ONLY WISH I COULD HAVE FOUND IT IN MY HEART, TO HAVE FORGIVEN HIM WHEN HE WAS ALIVE.

ONCE AGAIN, I SAY I AM VERY SORRY TO HAVE CAUSED YOU THIS MISERY AND HEARTACHE.

I SHALL DIE LOVING YOUR SON, AND YOU SHOULD FEEL CONTENT THAT HIS DEATH HAS BEEN REPAID.

GOODBYE
RUTH ELLIS

She blames herself, David, his friends the Findlaters, and even the pen used to write this emotionally charged letter is no good. Ruth was an obsessively jealous person and out of her many visits to the Buckinghamshire countryside during their affair, precious few were other than to check up on her lover. She knew that Mrs Cook would not approve of her, and David would reinforce her view by organising only clandestine visits to his Penn home. His stepfather had built him his own flat at their sumptuous country home, The Old Park, complete with his own front door, garages for his precious cars and a live-in nanny.

It paints an odd picture, David, a professed womaniser, living at home and cared for by a nanny who had looked after him as a boy and having to sneak his lover into his flat or check that his mum wasn't in the Crown pub at Penn before taking Ruth there for a weekend drinking session.

When they could escape somewhere as passionate lovers they would go on what can only be called drink and sex sprees that could last for some days. They would find neutral ground by going to a hotel, both drinking to excess in sessions that would usually end in violent rages and physical aggression towards each other. Ruth's bitterness always stemmed from her obsession that David was unfaithful to her, and she was right. Ruth also had an on-going relationship with a man called Desmond Cussen. In turn, he was very jealous of David, as David was of him, but Ruth would claim to David he was just a friend helping her with a place to live in London. It was Desmond who chauffeured Ruth on her frequent visits to Penn, or the Bull in Gerrards Cross to spy on David. It was also Desmond who drove her to the Magdala public house in Hampstead on that fateful Easter Sunday afternoon, a gun in her handbag. It has also been alleged that it was Desmond who taught Ruth to shoot in woods at Gerrards Cross and gave her the gun that was used to kill David.

It has remained a mystery how such a small, albeit ragingly angry woman was able to aim five shots so accurately into David Blakely, particularly as the gun, a double-action revolver with a heavy recoil action, needed to be reset each time it was fired. Ruth's tiny hands would have made it difficult for her to hold and steady such a cumbersome weapon.

There is no question she did this, but was she trained to do so in Buckinghamshire woodland? If this was the case, it adds a further chilling element of cold-blooded preparation to the undoubtedly premeditated murder of David Blakely. Perhaps this thought claws something back from claims of an injustice against Ruth Ellis.

So what drove this relationship along and why was Ruth hidden from David's family in Penn yet regarded by the landlord of the local pub, the Crown, as David's current girlfriend?

Before Ruth Ellis (formerly Neilson) was to become involved in her torrid love affair with David, she had already had a child when she was 18, after a brief relationship with a French Canadian man called Clare who returned home to his wife and children in 1944. She named the boy Clare Andrea Neilson after his dad, but he was always known as Andy. The man who changed her name from Neilson to Ellis was George Ellis, an alcoholic dentist whose first marriage had collapsed because of his heavy drinking. He was 42 and Ruth was 24 when they married on 8th November 1950. By 1951 Ruth was pregnant and gave birth to her daughter Georgina. George was a violent drunk and so the marriage was a disaster. Also, Ruth began to exhibit the intense jealousy that was to blight her later relationship with David Blakely at Penn. George ended up in hospital with his drinking problem and Ruth would accuse him of having sexual relationships with the female staff and other patients. Ruth's elder

The Crown at Penn, David Blakely's local pub

sister Muriel played a large part in looking after her children whilst Ruth established her nightclub hostess career in seedy London clubs, leaving George behind as a lost cause.

A long hot summer in 1953 began the chain of events that was to lead to the Buckinghamshire connection in Ruth's life and again after her death. It was also a most exciting and passionate time for her, mixing with the new, expensive, upper class world of motor-racing. Young men, glamorous racing drivers, many famous names, contrasted starkly with the older, boring, seedy businessmen she normally mixed with in her hostess work at Carroll's Club. They had their own Steering Wheel Club in London's Hyde Park area, but they would wander over to drink in the more exciting environment of Carroll's, where they could flirt with the girls and more. Ruth liked their company. However, she wasn't sure about one man who wandered in towards the end of that long summer. He was David Moffatt Drummond Blakely.

It certainly wasn't love at first sight between Ruth and, in her view, this rather pompous public school boy with a condescending manner. 'Too hoity-toity by far,' she has been recorded as saying.

Later the same year, they were to meet again in yet a different club. A local club owner had offered Ruth the opportunity to take on one of his establishments called the Little Club, and make it her own project, complete with three hostesses to manage. She also got a two bedroomed flat above the premises. She moved in with her son Andy, leaving daughter Georgie with her sister Muriel.

Unbeknown to Ruth, David Blakely happened to be a member of that club already. It is also claimed that David was the first person she served there. Both were surprised at this unexpected meeting and within a matter of weeks they would be having a passionate affair.

Ruth was 27 and David was 24 years old.

David's mother Anne Blakely had remarried in 1941 after divorcing his father, a doctor. His stepfather was one of Britain's foremost racing drivers, Humphrey Wyndham Cook, who had encouraged David's racing career by giving him a second-hand sports car for his 21st birthday.

Like Ruth, David had past relationships that were complicated and still part of his life. In 1951 he had met Anthony and Carole Findlater through a racing car sale. David was 21, Carole 27 and her husband, who was called Ant for short, was 29. David had an affair with Carole and wanted to run away with her. Carole told Ant of the affair but due to both men's love of racing cars this revelation failed to dent their friendship. These are the Findlaters that Ruth was referring to in her Holloway Prison letter to Mrs Cook. Ruth always maintained they conspired against her and protected David from her finding out the truth about his womanising and double-crossing whilst she was with him.

During the time that David met Ruth in the Little Club and began sleeping with her in the flat above, he became formally engaged to a Miss Linda Dawson, an event her father, a wealthy manufacturer from Huddersfield, had announced in the *London Times* on 11th November 1953. By this time, however, David was a month into a passionate affair with Ruth, who herself was still married to the absent George. David would also sleep with other women whenever the opportunity presented itself.

A promising career opportunity as a management trainee at the Hyde Park Hotel, set up by his stepfather, was lost when David was sacked after a major row with their banqueting manager. His mother took him on a world cruise to unwind and then back to the family home in Penn. Here he got a job as works manager at a small engineering firm called Silicone Pistons, just off Hazlemere Road. It was at that time that his stepfather organised a separate flat for David in one wing of The Old Park, the Cooks' new home in Hammersley Lane. One thing was certain, Ruth would not be taken home to meet Mum and stepdad in Penn and David had no intention of becoming stepfather to Ruth's two children. It was a sexual adventure for them both that would end in tragedy for him and infamy for her.

The frustration Ruth felt at being David's guilty secret from his mother was brought well and truly home to her on New Year's Eve 1954.

David collected Ruth from London to take her down to the Crown at Penn for a New Year drink. The landlord, George Edward Swarbrick Bessley, knew Ruth from previous visits and regarded her as David's girlfriend. That evening, however, just as David reached the pub, he noticed his mother going in and quickly carried on driving, pulling in further down the road at the Red Lion. Some of David's work colleagues from Silicone Pistons were there so Ruth and David joined them for a few drinks.

They then drove back up the road to the Crown. David left Ruth in the car while he checked if his mother was still there. She was. He wished her a Happy New Year, kissed her and then sneaked a drink out to Ruth in the car. This made Ruth determined not to put up with her hidden status for much longer. Things had got to change.

Whilst David was not a faithful lover, nor was Ruth. She loved him but while he travelled the world living the adventurous lifestyle of a racing car driver, she began an affair with Desmond Cussen, an older man. The year was 1954, Cussen was 33 and Ruth was now 28 with little more than a year of her life left before the hangman, Albert Pierrepoint, executed her.

Cussen resented David's affair with Ruth and her obvious affection towards him. But as Desmond was besotted by Ruth he'd do anything for her and that included driving Ruth to various venues in Buckinghamshire to see what her other lover was doing. Ruth suspected that David was having an affair with a married woman close to his home and she became known in their frequent and violent rows on the subject as 'the lady at Penn' or 'the attraction'.

Ruth was convinced that she was only taken to the Crown when David knew that 'the lady at Penn' would not be there. David worked locally and enjoyed drinking in the Crown at lunchtimes and Ruth was convinced that this attractive, older married woman would be with him.

Ruth received a telephone call from David shortly after the New Year's incident to say he was in the Crown, it was just closing, but he wouldn't be coming up to London to see her as planned as he was having an early night and staying at home. Ruth did not believe a word of this, but said goodbye, grabbed her coat and instructed Desmond to drive her to Penn. She wanted to catch David out with this other woman on his own doorstep. His car was not in the garage so Desmond drove her to a nearby house that David had once carelessly referred to as the Penn Nightclub. They waited and watched. They saw David leave around 2.30 am and then silently left. The next day Ruth asked him about his early night but said nothing about the fact that she knew it was a lie.

By 10th January 1955, despite more passionate hotel sessions, the rows, fighting and jealousy reached such a pitch that Ruth threatened to confront the the lady at Penn, and to tell David's mother all about her own role in David's life. David was terrified and even more so when a telegram arrive at Silicone Pistons which read:

PERSONAL MR D BLAKELY SYLICUM PISTONS LTD PENN BUCKS HAVEN'T YOU GOT THE GUTS TO SAY GOODBYE TO MY FACE – RUTH

David had some thinking to do. Would Ruth really do this? Probably. With Ruth's threat hanging in the air, they resumed their tempestuous relationship, staying in London hotels every night and embarking on a massive binge of sex, drinking and arguing that lasted from 27th January until 6th February. When David took Ruth back to Desmond's flat that Sunday evening, the violence between them bubbled up once more over the lady at Penn, leaving Ruth covered in bruises and refusing to give David his car keys and David with a black eye, claiming Ruth had tried to knife him. David phoned his friends Ant and Clive to come and help him, which they did. David made a run for it while Ruth was occupied with his friends. She followed and a huge row in the street erupted as Ruth sat in his precious car, refusing to move. David shouted 'she won't let me go' over and over again.

He could not know how true that statement was going to be.

Ruth was distracted again by Ant and Clive, allowing David to drive away, leaving Ruth lying the road in a drunken attempt to stop anyone else leaving. Much later that evening Ruth was on her way to Penn once again, chauffeured, of course, by the ever reliable Desmond. Arriving at The Old Park in the early hours of Monday morning, worse for wear and with a damaged ankle from the earlier fracas, Ruth hobbled down the long driveway and hammered on the door of his flat. David's nanny answered, followed by David in his pyjamas, who, on seeing Ruth, turned and fled out of the back door into his car and drove off, only coming back when the coast was clear.

Ruth told Desmond later that night that she wanted to return to Penn, '… to get an apology from that bastard'.

So began the hunt again the next day with Desmond telephoning Silicone Pistons but David wouldn't come to the phone. Again he drove Ruth to Buckinghamshire and, as luck would have it, spotted David's car outside the Bull at Gerrards

The entrance leading to David's home, The Old Park in Penn

Cross. While Ruth waited, Desmond went in, grabbed David and said, 'Come on you bastard, outside.'

A row erupted with Ruth accusing David of breaking her ankle and threatening that she was going to see his mother and tell her about it. Desmond continued to insult David but violence was avoided; David walked to his car and drove away. Ruth set off with Desmond to confront David's mother at The Old Park. For whatever motive, Desmond talked her out of it and they returned to London. Later red carnations arrived for Ruth with a card that read 'Sorry darling, I love you, David'.

Ruth's obsession with the lady at Penn was not to be bought off with flowers, so the journeys to spy on David at Penn continued, whether it was to his workplace or the Crown, or the house where 'the attraction' lived. Things came to a head when Ruth and Desmond waited all night outside the house in question. David had hidden his car round the back of the Crown just down the road. When David left the lady at 9 am in the morning, he saw Desmond's car and hurried back inside. Desmond knocked on the door and Ruth confronted David, who said he had to go to work and swiftly left.

Ruth was invited in and the women compared stories over a cup of coffee, Ruth reporting later that her rival had apologised as she didn't know about David and Ruth's special relationship. Ruth had a result and was happy. Happy enough to go to the Crown with Desmond, who rang Silicone Pistons inviting David to join them. Surprisingly he did, accompanied by a work colleague and 'the lady at Penn', no less. It seemed she and Ruth now had an understanding.

Later, when David had returned to work and while Ruth was still drinking in the Crown, Desmond drove the short distance to Silicone Pistons and spoke to David, almost apologising for spying on him, and they shook hands. This was, however, the calm before the storm.

Ruth found she was pregnant.

She also suspected David had not given up his affair and again the team of Desmond and Ruth would turn up without warning at the Crown to catch David out. They found the lady at Penn was still very much in his life. The arguments continued and on 28th March Ruth miscarried. At her trial she said of that time, 'David got very, very violent. I do not know whether that caused the miscarriage or not, but he did thump me in the tummy.' David's friends Carole and Ant Findlater regarded the pregnancy as a trick by Ruth to force David into marriage.

It was Easter Sunday, 10th April 1955, Desmond was in attendance as always and after more drinking it was clear that Ruth wanted a final showdown. David was staying with the Findlaters in Hampstead. At around 8.45 pm he had popped along to the Magdala pub with his other friend Clive to get Carole some cigarettes. Ruth was also out that evening, again driven by Desmond, but this time she had a .38 Smith and Wesson in her handbag and more anger in her heart than one can imagine.

They saw David's car parked by the pub. Desmond stopped and Ruth, eschewing her usual vanity, put on her glasses, got out, and went over to the pub. Desmond drove off. She did not have long to wait until David and Clive came out and were about to get back into their car. Ruth shouted David's name. They didn't seem to hear. She shouted it again, 'David!'

He looked, there was Ruth with a gun pointing at him; he ran.

Ruth fired two shots and he was hit. He was wounded and tried to run but Ruth shot again and he fell. She fired once more and then walked up to where he lay, firing a fifth shot at point-blank range. There was blood, screaming and confusion. It is claimed that Ruth pointed the gun at her head, then, lowering the weapon,

The Bucks Free Press

Incorporating The South Bucks Free Press,
High Wycombe, Maidenhead & Marlow Journal
and South Oxfordshire Gazette

Established 1856

Circulating throughout Buckinghamshire and in
the adjoining Counties of Middlesex, Berkshire,
Oxfordshire and Hertfordshire.

No. 5130   99th YEAR   FRIDAY, APRIL 15, 1955   THREEPENCE

WOMAN MODEL ACCUSED OF KILLING PENN MAN

Sequel To Discovery Outside A London Inn

GUNSHOT WOUND ALLEGED

A 28-YEARS-OLD model, Ruth Ellis, of Egerton-gardens, Kensington, was charged at Hampstead on Monday with the murder the previous night of David Moffatt Drummond Blakely, whose address is stated to be at the Old Park, Penn, Bucks.

She was remanded in custody until Wednesday, April 20.

Mr. Blakely, aged 25, was found on Sunday night outsisde a public house in South Hill Park, London, N.W. He had a gunshot wound.

Mr. David Blakely

Detective Chief Inspector Davies said that he saw Ellis at Hampstead police station and told her that, as a result of a post-mortem examination on Mr. Blakely, she would be charged with murdering him. When cautioned she said. "I understand." When the charge was read over to her she said, "Thanks".

"Prisoner has made a statement which it is not proposed to put in at this stage," said Chief Inspector Davies.

Asked if she wanted to ask Chief Inspector Davies anything Ellis said "No".

A certificate for legal aid was granted.

The hearing lasted four minutes.

Inquest Adjourned

The inquest on Mr Blakely, which was opened on Tuesday was adjourned by the St. Pancras Coroner, Mr. R. I. Milne, until May 10.

Evidence of identification was given by Mr. Anthony Seaton Findlater, an engineer, of Tanzaroad Hampstead. He said that Mr. Blakely, who lived at the Old Park, Penn, Bucks, was spending the week-end with him.

"He went out to buy a bottle of beer," said Mr. Findlater, "That was the last I saw of him"

Detective Chief Inspector Leslie Davies, told the Coroner that a woman named Ruth Ellis had been charged with the murder of Mr. Blakely.

A pathologist, Dr. A. C. Hunt, said that death was due to shock and haemorrhage due to a gunshot wound.

REFEREE IS HURT JUST BEFORE GAME

SHORTLY after returning from his honeymoon, and a few hours before he was due to referee the final of the High Wycombe Challenge Cup competition at High Wycombe on Good Friday, Mr. Roy Boyles, of 259 West Wycombe-road, High Wycombe, was injured in a motor car accident at Beaconsfield.

He was taken to High Wycombe War Memorial Hospital with head and knee injuries after a collision between the car in which he was travelling and a car in which were Mr. and Mrs.

LEFT LITTER ON ROADSIDE

Wycombe Man Fined At Beaconsfield

A pile of litter which he found by the roadside at Potkiln-lane, Beaconsfield, on March 14, was described by Police-constable J. Bradshaw at Beaconsfield magistrates court on Tuesday.

The litter, he said, included old clothing, paper, coconut matting, old shoes, and pieces of carpet.

For leaving the litter Herbert Saunders, of 80 Totteridge-avenue, High Wycombe, was fined £2.

Sir Norman Kendal, the chairman, said that people must be made to realise that they could not dump their rubbish where they pleased and spoil the beauties of Beaconsfield.

Saunders wrote to the court apologising.

THEY WANT THEIR VILLAGE TIDY

The arrest of Ruth Ellis made the front page of the local newspaper on 15th April 1955. (© Bucks Free Press and reproduced with permission of The British Library) fired at the pavement. There were plenty of witnesses, indeed one was injured slightly from the final ricocheted bullet.

Off-duty police constable Alan Thompson was in the pub at the time. He hurried out and calmly approached Ruth who stood holding the gun in both hands. It is reported that she said to him, 'Will you call the police?' He replied, 'I am the police.' Ruth is then reported to have said, 'Will you please arrest me?'

Ruth Ellis made a statement admitting to the shooting of David Blakely and she was charged with murder at 12.30 pm on Easter Monday, 11th April 1955 and remanded to Holloway.

The trial began on Monday 20th June 1955 and lasted only a day and a half. Ruth pleaded not guilty.

Her defence hoped that they could show a woman driven to the edge and to manslaughter rather than murder. The jury took only 23 minutes to return a guilty verdict on the second day of the trial. Placing the ceremonial black cap on his head, Mr Justice Havers had no choice but to pronounce the death sentence, to which Ruth replied, 'Thank you.'

Just 24 days from the pronouncement of the death sentence in court it was carried out at Holloway Prison.

From Holloway, she had asked her mother to place red carnations and one white carnation on David's grave at Penn.

The executioner Albert Pierrepoint entered Ruth's cell at 9 am on Wednesday 13th July 1955; it was a matter of no more than a dozen seconds before she was dead.

Both parties to this passionate, violent and turbulent affair were now dead. David buried in the churchyard of the Holy Trinity church in his home village of Penn in the county of Buckinghamshire and Ruth buried in the unconsecrated grounds of Holloway Prison.

There it might have ended but there is another twist to their tortuous relationship that brought Ruth closer to David once again.

At the beginning of 1970, Holloway Prison underwent a major rebuilding programme and it meant that bodies had to be reinterred. If relatives were available they were contacted and asked for their preferred burial location. Ruth's son Andy, now 26, wished to unite his mum and David once more by requesting that Ruth should be buried with him in Penn.

The vicar of the parish, Oscar Muspratt, taking account of the wishes of David's family, refused to allow this. Not deterred, Andy found a place for his mother as close to David as possible; this was to be 4 miles away in St Mary's cemetery in Amersham, where she now rests.

Ruth had never been able to take on the true name of her parents as she had been registered as Neilson after her musician father's professional name rather than Hornby, the real family name. Then she became Ellis after her marriage to George. Finally, she had longed to become Ruth Blakely but it wasn't to be. In Amersham, as close as she'll ever be to David, she has, in her final resting place, become Ruth Hornby, the name she should have had in the very beginning in that year of 1926 in the seaside town of Rhyl.

Would it have made a difference? Probably not.

Ruth's headstone at Amersham was smashed and never replaced; her grave remains unmarked. (© Mirror Pix)

GEORGE – THE SUMMERTIME GHOST OF EDLESBOROUGH

———————— ❀ ————————

Do ye believe in ghosts, said she,
And from whence such things stem?
No, I replied, I don't believe.
But I'm still afraid of them!

(Anon)

Ghosts are amongst the most widespread of all paranormal phenomena and have always featured somewhere in the stories, legends and experiences of every culture yet discovered. For would-be ghost hunters the difficulty of trying to capture them on film and sound leads others, more sceptical, to doubt their existence at all. But many of us fear the horror of being haunted or cursed and the spooky, eerie presence of any apparition or spectral manifestation, especially if it enters our home. Reports abound of the cold chills and shivers that are said to be experienced in the presence of a haunting or perhaps the malicious mischief said to be wrought by a poltergeist.

But it is not always like this. Indeed, we may be encountering more supernatural and spiritual beings than we will ever know. That brief feeling that someone just brushed past you although you are alone in the room, that glimpse out of the corner of your eye of something moving past the window, but you can't quite place what you saw. Perhaps a premonition that, with hindsight, now makes you realise that you should have trusted your own feelings at the time.

Substitute *presence* for *ghost* and possibly you may agree that you can recall the sense of something or someone being close by, yet nothing tangible actually appearing. Another time, there might be a brief image of something that does appear real, something that only has a fleeting existence and quickly reduces to nothing, this is known as a *shade*. And then perhaps you are ready for the next step, which is when you will see a *ghost* – an apparition, the perceived spirit of a dead person or animal. Let me take you to the tiny Buckinghamshire village of Edlesborough on the Bucks/Bedfordshire border and introduce you to George who has emerged from presence and shade to become the resident ghost of Swallowfields.

Swallowfields is a cosy family home which has been painstakingly converted from what was once a barn. The original farm, built around 1580, was called Charity Farm and something must have happened in its long and colourful past that could provide the key to explain why George still lives there today.

George is not his real name, unless by coincidence. It has been conferred upon him by those who regularly witness his appearances and now see him as a regular part of life at Swallowfields. I have no doubt that his true identity will be revealed one day, but several mysteries remain to be solved before that can be possible.

Swallowfields is now one of four barns clustered around the original farmhouse, which during 1974 and 1975 became modern, attractive homes within a secluded courtyard in a much sought after area. But in 1974 when Brian and Christine Plantan planned their dream home it was no more than a shell, a large barn – battered and bruised by four centuries of weather and its constant use for the storage of farm implements – with a raised area of floor for threshing the harvest.

They lived in a caravan in the stable yard with their three Jack Russell dogs, Tinkle, Widdle and Susie, waiting for the day the builders would move out and they could move in. By June 1975 they had their wish, and Christine's mother Joan came to stay with them to help sort out their new home.

There was lots more to be done, especially to make Swallowfields more secure as there was no side gate and no back porch – you stepped straight from the kitchen out to the back step – but Tinkle, Widdle and Susie were good guard dogs and always alerted the Plantans to visitors.

On several occasions, however, during those summer days, Christine had been aware of someone walking past the window in

Swallowfields at Edlesborough, where George is often seen on his way to the old barn entrance

the front of the house and heading round to the back door, but on checking, no one was there. It transpired that her mother had also been aware of a figure walking past this same window and making for the back of the house, and she had gone to the back door on several occasions only to discover no one was there.

This went on for a number of months and they both realised that each time the figure had gone past Tinkle, Widdle and Susie had not responded in any way at all. They were completely oblivious of any unexpected visitor intruding upon their territory – a privilege not extended to the postman, milkman or indeed most other callers.

The summer of 1975 passed, Christine's mother had gone home, and little more was said on the subject, particularly as Brian had always made fun of them and dismissed their feelings of a *presence*. In retrospect, however, this had moved rapidly into the stage of being a classic case of *shade,* the fleeting glance of what appeared to be a real image moving silently before them, each of them witnessing this phenomenon individually before sharing what they had seen with each other.

Winter approached and Christine was busy with the work of caring for their horses and no more such occurrences were experienced. Even when her mother stayed with them over the Christmas period, neither had any more glimpses of such a figure passing by their front window.

It seemed it had just been a brief episode now to be forgotten.

After Christmas and into the new year of 1976, Christine and Brian had a request from a friend to help a young lad find lodgings in Edlesborough as he'd just landed a job nearby. They were happy to help out and offer accommodation at Swallowfields itself.

So it was that Robin came to stay with the Plantan family. He worked a shift pattern so did not keep regular hours and would often be in the house alone in the mornings, waking up late and making himself a late breakfast or brunch. Christine would be up the stable yard most of the morning and was also busy giving riding lessons in the afternoons, whilst Brian was away from the crack of dawn until dusk delivering animal feeds.

Spring passed swiftly and as the summer weather approached, Robin found himself checking the back door during the late morning or early afternoon to see who it was had just gone past the front window, heading for the back of the house. Again, when the dogs were about, they didn't bark or show any interest. He mentioned it to Christine, who laughed and replied, 'Didn't I tell you about our ghost?' Although said in jest, she now half-believed it herself – was Swallowfields haunted?

Then came an event that began to change the whole experience as *shade*, became *ghost*.

One summer day when Christine came down from the stable yard to the house, Robin greeted her with some surprise, so Christine asked if he was okay. Robin asked her if she had been in the front hall earlier. Christine explained that she had been giving riding lessons and had not been back to the house since she left early that morning while he was still asleep.

Why, she wanted to know, what has happened?

Robin explained that as he walked from his bedroom across the small landing to the bathroom, he saw a figure standing in the front hall wearing a brown outdoor coat and assumed it was her.

He didn't speak because he was only in his pyjamas and needed the toilet with some urgency so he shot across the landing straight into the bathroom.

Christine explained that she had not come back to the house until this moment, and did not possess a brown coat. So who had he seen standing in the front hall?

Robin moved out that year, having found himself a flat.

Again that summer Christine would experience the figure moving past her window, heading for the back of the house, and again there would be no reaction from Tinkle, Widdle and Susie and there would be nobody waiting outside. However, these continuing brief glimpses allowed Christine to built up a clearer picture of the shape moving soundlessly past the window in broad daylight. He was clearly male with long blonde hair and wearing a brown coat which he clasped around his neck as if he was cold. His posture was one of leaning forward, giving the appearance of walking into a strong wind. But she could only see him from the waist up, as if he was walking at a lower level outside than the actual courtyard that now exists.

Brian had no sympathy for Christine's story and dismissed it as rubbish despite the experience related by Robin.

However, Christine and her mother when she occasionally came to stay were now fully aware of these unpredictable, swift appearances and couldn't disregard them so easily. Then came another event that confirmed that something very extraordinary was indeed occurring.

During that same summer, when the sightings were running at as many as three times a week of this figure going past the window, Christine was working up at the stable when a young girl she had employed to assist her had gone down to Swallowfields to use the toilet. However, she immediately returned to the yard to say that there was a man waiting by the back door so she thought she ought to come straight back and tell Christine as there was no one in the house at the time. Christine asked her what he looked like, and she described him as tall, with long blonde hair and wearing a heavy brown coat and dark brown trousers and he looked quite young.

Christine didn't know whether to be relieved or worried, but he had gone by the time she went to check. It was from this time that Christine and Joan nicknamed the figure 'George' and vowed to try and find out more about their own Swallowfields ghost even if Brian thought they were mad.

George might appear for three or four consecutive days and then nothing was seen for a month, and he never appeared in the winter. The sightings run from June to September each year right up to the present moment of writing. Husband Brian remained sceptical for a long time, but in the summer of 1999 he and Christine were in their front room, when he suddenly got up from his chair and headed for the back door. Christine asked him where he was off to, and he replied that somebody had just walked past the window and they were coming to the back door. George, it seems, felt it was about time to introduce himself to Brian.

Brian returned to report that no one was there. Tinkle, Widdle and Susie were no longer around, of course, but had been replaced by Gladys, Mabel, Daisy and Wilfred, who, like their predecessors, did not bark or show any reaction to someone being outside.

The transformation from *presence,* to *shade* and into *ghost,* was now starting to occur.

Christine was sitting in the front room one recent summer day and the sky went very black as if there was going to be a storm but it was extremely humid and she had left the back door open. She felt someone behind her, and thinking it was Brian, turned around to tell him not to creep up on her like that – and there was George.

There was no feeling of apprehension or fall in temperature as most people are led to believe happens when you are close to a ghost, in fact, on the contrary, he stood quite still smiling at Christine. He was tall with long fair hair down to his collar, smooth and slightly wavy. He was wearing a light brown smock with a paler, almost yellow shirt with a large collar underneath the smock. On top he had a long brown coat down to his knees and dark brown trousers … the image faded and he was gone.

So who is George and what happened to him?

It seems we need to return once more to Charity Farm and see if a connection exists between the original barn and George's continuing association with it. Also there are some physical clues that were kept as souvenirs when the conversion work took place in 1974. When the original barn roof was repaired and replaced, the builders found two small pieces of wood, tucked away in the original joists. Both pieces of wood had names and dates carved

The mysterious pieces of wood discovered during the barn conversion work in 1974

on them, possibly by the carpenter or roofer employed to carry out storm damage repairs. Perhaps they hold some answers to what had happened at Charity Farm and why George still lives there.

One piece has the name William A Berd and the dates 1809/1810 carved deeply into it, also a JxGWB. The other has the inscription WBIW 1810. Can these help us solve the mystery of Swallowfields ghost? Is George, perhaps, really William?

According to the county records, Charity Farm employed casual farm workers who were able to earn their keep rather than be a drain on the parish poor relief or the workhouse. Upwards of 30 to 40 men and boys would work on the farm, especially in the summer for haymaking and for the harvest time, which started in late July and went on until the last week of August.

This certainly fits with George's preference for summer hauntings. We also know that Swallowfields was originally a large barn with double doors just where George tends to stand or appear to head for. Also the farmyard outside the barn was at a lower level in the 18th and 19th centuries than it is today, so Swallowfields' modern house window is quite high, revealing only the top half of anyone walking past at the original farmyard level.

But why is he seen bent forward as if leaning against the wind whenever he passes by the window?

Investigations show that directly in front of where he is heading was an old lean-to porch area that would afford shelter from a sudden summer storm. Humid summer conditions can regularly produce what we tend to call electric storms. George wasn't heading for the back door at all, but straight ahead to this lean-to which is now incorporated into next door's house wall and no longer in evidence except for the original slanting roof line off the end of the house. Also he would be heading directly into the prevailing wind at that point.

It also appears that there was an August storm in 1809, described by a contemporary observer as 'One of the most extraordinary storms ever remembered. The damage done has been enormous'. Workers on hayricks were blown off and barn roofs were damaged, some people being injured or killed by falling timbers and slates. George may well have been one of those killed on his way to seek shelter from this sudden storm. He was likely to have been what was called a sojourner – a temporary resident who visits and revisits at specific times to work on seasonal projects, or perhaps even receive instruction in a trade or craft so he can become more skilled. Perhaps the carved initials were the work of the carpenter who was employed on the extensive repairs to the barn during that year and early the next. It is possible, of course, that it is the carpenter himself that passes by that window and into the old barn area. The mystery of George, the summertime ghost of Edelsborough, remains to be solved.

'DON'T LET MY MUSIC DIE'

❁

M iss Lilian Pretoria Marks felt life was passing her by. What future was there for a young lady working as a grocery assistant on thirty shillings a week in High Wycombe?

It was 1920, the Great War was over, and fun times should be around the corner, not just shelves stacked with groceries and the promise of the local 'palais' at the weekend. An excursion to the Grand cinema in Desborough Road to see a Pearl White adventure or a visit to the Jolly Butcher in The Narrows was nearest life got to excitement until, at the end of August that year, she came across a bizarre advertisement in the *Bucks Free Press* that caught her imagination. '*Young ladies, not under sixteen, must be over 5 foot 6 inches, well built, full figure, or slim build. Applicants below height specified, please state qualifications as to appearance, etc. Required for highly paid specialised work, indoors or out. Applications from all classes entertained, as duties will be taught. Write, in first instance, to 'Snap', 'Free Press' Office, Wycombe.*'

Writing back could do no harm and she could learn a new skill. She fitted all the personal qualifications, so why not? She wrote and she received a reply that requested her to visit a house in Furlong Road, Bourne End any evening after 6 pm. This was, after all, the new decade of adventure and excitement following the privations of war, so why not live for today and see what this highly paid job was all about.

After a long weekend thinking about it, she decided that come Monday evening after work, she'd pay a visit. So it was that on Monday 6th September 1920 young Miss Marks, grocery assistant of High Wycombe, found herself outside this Bourne End address contemplating the possibility of being involved in something that would change her life for ever.

The door opened and a clean-shaven man in his early thirties introduced himself as George Bailey and invited her in. He wasted no time in enthusiastically explaining what lay behind his unusual advertisement. Ushering Miss Marks into the front room, he told her that he was setting up a musical academy in nearby Little Marlow. He had invented a new way of learning and teaching music and if she studied his system hard for two weeks she could then advertise it and take on her own pupils. He wanted to recruit around seven or eight young ladies to be his pupils at the new academy so they could become proficient enough to spread his remarkable invention of a new musical notation to others. This would revolutionise the teaching of music, he claimed, as his system did not use sharps or flats and was written in one key.

To his question of whether she was at all musical she asked if he meant singing or piano?

'Piano,' he replied.

He assured her that he could teach her all that she needed to know. He then moved on to the part of the advert that referred to her build and asked her to take off her hat and stand against the door so he could examine her figure more clearly. Miss Marks took off her hat and unfastened her coat. Bailey also took hold of her hands and examined them. Clearly satisfied, he said he would pay her three guineas a week. She should give in her notice to the grocery store, inform her parents of this new opportunity and write to him again when she was ready to start as his pupil alongside the seven or eight other young ladies he expected to employ at his Little Marlow Musical Academy.

He also added that it would be more practical for her to stay overnight on two or three occasions a week with some of the other young ladies under his tuition so it could be a proper learning experience and not broken up by long journeys between Wycombe and Marlow.

Miss Marks promised to consult her parents and let him know. In the second week of September she received a letter from Mr Bailey, dated September 10th, thanking her profusely for her visit and inviting her to start tuition with him in the week commencing 27th September. The letter asked her to bring all she needed to stay overnight at his new academy and to arrive for an early start so he could draw up a suitable timetable of instruction. The final agreement was for Miss Marks to meet George Bailey with her overnight bag on the morning of Wednesday 29th September in Little Marlow.

Complete with businessman's bowler hat and raincoat, George Bailey greeted his new pupil as arranged and took her to his 'academy'. This turned out to be Barn Cottage in Little Marlow.

As he politely ushered her into the drawing room, Miss Marks felt much more at ease to be introduced to two other young lady pupils, a Miss Winifred Field and a Miss Gladys Edwards. This certainly looked as if Mr Bailey's promise that she would be a pupil with other young ladies was indeed correct, and in the corner of the room was a piano. Bailey wanted to start immediately, so without showing Miss Marks to her room, he began explaining to his class of three the nature of his newly invented musical system. Part of the instruction involved Miss Field playing the piano from traditional music notation whilst he explained on paper sheets how his invention would change this and make it easy for anyone to learn and teach music. All three concentrated on George Bailey's enthusiastic instruction until around 1 pm that day.

The advertisement that George Bailey placed in the local newspaper on 27th August 1920. (© Bucks Free Press)

The only brief distraction that morning was the sound of a young child talking in an adjoining room and also Miss Marks thought she caught a glimpse of a dress or possibly an apron passing by the drawing room door, which was slightly ajar.

So there were others living in this house, she thought.

Anyway, instruction was over for the morning and it was arranged that Miss Field and Miss Edwards should leave and return the next morning for the second tuition session and that Miss Marks would stay overnight as planned. Bailey asked Miss Marks what arrangements she had made for lunch but she said she had left it up to him what should be done. He then gave her four shillings to buy lunch in Marlow and was very clear that she should not under any circumstances return to Barn Cottage until 7 pm that evening. Miss Marks set off into Marlow and spent the afternoon and early evening there, waiting to return and unpack her portmanteau. It was rather a long time to wait but, so far, things were turning out just as Mr Bailey had promised and she was excited.

At 7 pm sharp, Lilian Marks knocked on the door of Barn Cottage. George Bailey greeted her and showed her into the dining room. He explained that whilst she had been out, two more pupils had arrived from Scotland and being very tired after their long journey had gone to bed. In fact there should also have been a third pupil arriving but for some reason she had not done so. Anyway, tuition would begin the next morning and now there would be five pupils, possibly six if the missing lady turned up. The academy was taking shape.

George Bailey then picked up Miss Marks' case and led the way to her room so she could settle in before supper. She heard a child crying in the next room and called down to Mr Bailey, asking if she should go and see what was wrong. 'No, I will see to it,' he replied immediately, making it clear she was not to investigate.

She unpacked and heard him next door soothing the child, who did eventually stop crying. She went back downstairs and had supper in the dining room with Bailey, who occasionally popped outside to see if the missing pupil was to be seen. He would not talk about the child except to say, rather mysteriously, that if the child cried again, he would have to go through Miss Marks' bedroom to comfort it. He did not reply to her inquiry as to why that was necessary when he could use the main door as before rather than cross her room to the interconnecting door.

Miss Marks joined him outside on the lawn for about three-quarters of an hour, both looking out for another young lady on her way to Barn Cottage but no one came. It was coming up for 9 pm, so she decided it was time for her to go to bed.

He said he would stay up until 11 pm in case the new pupil had caught the last train to Bourne End. From her room, Miss Marks heard Mr Bailey going up and down the stairs and about 11 pm he shouted upstairs that the other girl had not arrived.

Lilian went to secure her door but found it was not possible to lock it. She could comfort herself with the knowledge that two other young ladies were in the house and everything he had promised so far had happened. She was, however, puzzled about the child and her brief glimpse of a woman passing the door. Was he married? She blew out her candle and tried to sleep after what was turning out to be quite a strange adventure.

Moonlight streamed thought her window and, half asleep, Lilian was aware of the latch on her bedroom door slowly being lifted. Creeping past her bed was George Bailey, wearing an overcoat over his pants. He made straight for the child's bedroom. Miss Marks did not know what to do. He had said he was going to pass through her room to check on the child, so once more he had done exactly what he had told her. She was probably worrying over nothing.

A little time elapsed and George Bailey reappeared in her room and whispered, 'Miss Marks, have I disturbed you?'

Lilian Marks said nothing, she didn't know what to say.

George Bailey went to the side of her bed and once more asked if he had disturbed her as the child had cried out. Miss Marks knew this to be a lie because she would have heard the child had it cried. She was now worried, and said to him, 'No it has not or I should have heard.'

Bailey, ignoring her comment, said, 'I am going to ask you a very great favour.'

She asked what it was, and he said it was '... to sit on the armchair behind the door.'

This was now seriously wrong thought Miss Marks, who began to panic. George Bailey questioned her about why she could not go back to sleep and she told him she could not whilst he remained in the room and he should go. He explained that he needed to ask her a question, which was 'What do you think of the cottage?'

This was now getting gravely out of hand, thought Miss Marks, and said she did not want to discuss this now and he should leave her room. Bailey ignored her protests and said, 'How would you like to be the mistress of the cottage?' Miss Marks was now agitated at the way this was going but he went on to add that he had come for one thing and if she couldn't decide it he would, and he sat on the side of her bed and then quickly tried to climb into bed with her and rape her.

She fought him but he was very strong and pushed her down each time she tried to prise him off. She struggled hard and did manage to escape from the bed and run to the window shouting help, but he pulled her back and said there was no one to hear her cries.

By now Miss Marks was hysterical and George Bailey was talking fast and furious, saying that he wanted her to be the mother of his children. She shouted he was to leave her alone and he had tricked her. He admitted that he had and there were no other young women in the house and he had come to her room solely for the purpose of having sexual intercourse with her so she could have his children. She said, in her confused state, 'It is ridiculous talking, that can never be.'

Throughout the night he made repeated attempts to assault her. She sustained bruises on her arms, chest and legs but he did not succeed in raping her.

Towards dawn, whilst Lilian Marks cowered terrified from him, he stayed silent and then he asked, 'Are you going to say anything about what happened?'

Miss Marks did not reply and he stayed there in glowering silence.

Dawn broke, Lilian not daring to sleep or antagonise him, Bailey sitting on the chair reflecting on what had happened.

By 8 am that morning, Lilian thought it was best to humour him so asked if she could go downstairs and prepare breakfast. He agreed she could do that while he went and had a shave.

Whether Lilian thought about making a run for it and changed her mind is not clear but she went downstairs and began to prepare breakfast as if nothing had happened. Bailey came downstairs for breakfast and he brought with him the young child whom she had heard crying, introducing her as Hollie, aged 3. He asked if the child looked like him.

Lilian said that she did. He explained that he was the child's uncle and Hollie's mother was unwell and living in Swindon. Lilian asked if he was married and Bailey said that he wasn't.

Breakfast over, Lilian cleared everything away and, as if nothing had happened, he asked her if she was ready to begin lessons. She explained she was too upset and shaken by events and wished to leave. Bailey then asked her to go to the village for him and buy some ham, fruit and cakes for lunch as he was expecting Miss Field and Miss Edwards at any moment. He gave her six shillings and sixpence to make the purchases.

Miss Marks went to her room rather than the village, got everything ready to leave and stayed there until 11.30 am when there was a knock at the door. Bailey answered it and admitted Miss Field and Miss Edwards. Quickly, Lilian put on her coat and slipped out the back door, heading for Cores End about 2 miles away, and went to the vicar's house, where she blurted out to a startled Reverend Allan all that had happened to her.

The vicar arranged for her to get home to her parents and once her father learnt about what had happened to his daughter, he cycled all the way from High Wycombe to Cores End to speak with Revd Allan.

Meanwhile around 3 pm that afternoon, the vicar went to Barn Cottage to talk to George Bailey. Bailey answered the door but claimed not to know a Miss Marks amongst his 'thirty pupils'. As Revd Allen prepared to leave, Bailey suddenly recalled a Miss Lilian Marks visiting him in a state of great distress. The vicar, however, had not mentioned to Bailey that Miss Marks' first name was Lilian. A distressed woman appearing on a doorstep would hardly reveal her first name to a total stranger. Revd Allan eventually met up with Mr Marks and they decided to report Bailey to the police.

It was now the afternoon of Thursday 30th September when Superintendent George Kirby from Wycombe and Inspector William West from Marlow received from Mr Marks a complaint of a serious assault against his daughter. Inspector West visited Barn Cottage the following morning to speak to Mr Bailey but there was no one there and the cottage was locked, although some windows were open upstairs.

Superintendent Kirby agreed to meet Inspector West the next morning, Saturday, at Barn Cottage to investigate further.

The truth about George Arthur Bailey was about to be unravelled. He was already under police surveillance by Marlow police, who had witnessed some thirty women calling at either Furlong Road or Barn Cottage in response to his advertisement. The cottage was just as Inspector West had found it on the Friday. They tried the doors but all were locked. However, the inspector climbed through a window, saw the front door key on the mat and was able to let Superintendent Kirby in.

No one was about and in fact the table was laid ready for tea with bread and jam, butter and cakes and some kind of pudding. This was hardly the scene of someone leaving in a panic knowing that they are likely to be reported for a serious sexual assault. Upstairs told a different story. In that back room where Lilian had heard the child crying were two camp beds, one of which was covered by a large counterpane and underneath that particular bed was what appeared to be a large bundle of sheets. When the officers investigated more closely they found the body of a young woman who had obviously been dead for a matter of days and whose flesh had some strange discolouration. They immediately arranged for two doctors to attend from Marlow and they both agreed it was death by poison. The cottage was sealed off as a crime scene and the hunt began immediately for George Bailey.

On Sunday 3rd October the famous Home Office pathologist Doctor Spilsbury carried out a post-mortem at the crime scene, removing the contents of the stomach for analysis at his London laboratory, but one thing was clear, the young woman was in an advanced stage of pregnancy, so there were now two victims of this tragic crime. The body was identified as Kate Lilian Bailey, aged 22, Bailey's wife of just over four years.

Bailey's real job was as a milkman for Mr Hall, the local dairyman, who had only recently taken him on. He had said he used to be a milkman for the Express Dairy Company, which was true. He did omit to tell Mr Hall, however, that in 1913 he was arrested and sentenced to six months hard labour for embezzling money from them. But there was lots more to be learnt about George Arthur Bailey, or should it be Arthur George Bailey, or even Ronald Gilbert Treherne, or perhaps Tremayne? He had been known to various police forces since 1908 when he had spent many spells in prison for fraud, forgery and embezzlement and had become an army deserter to add to his crimes. His unfortunate pregnant wife had also suffered committal to prison as a result of his crimes for passing the cheques he had forged, and young Hollie, whom Miss Marks wanted to comfort that terrible night, had been born in Winchester Prison.

Now Hollie's mother was dead, poisoned, so where was Hollie and more to the point her father, George Bailey?

It was, in fact, on Saturday evening, 2nd October, that PC Poole of Marlow police, who knew what Bailey looked like, spotted him and, together with Detective Sergeant Purdy of the Berkshire Constabulary, arrested him at Reading railway station. PC Poole had been sent there just in case Bailey turned up and he did. From Reading police station he was taken to Marlow, questioned and charged with the wilful murder of his wife, Kate Lilian Bailey.

But where was the child? Bailey had been to Swindon and left Hollie with his sister there and was apparently intending to return to Barn Cottage. On Monday 4th October Bailey appeared at Marlow Police Court for committal proceedings, was charged with murder and remanded to Oxford Prison. He made a second appearance at Marlow the next morning and was then sent back to Oxford Prison to await his trial at Aylesbury Crown Court.

The trial began in January 1921 and he pleaded not guilty but the witness evidence was overwhelming. Miss Field and Miss Edwards both appeared in court and described their dealings with Bailey, corroborating everything that Lilian Marks had said about the recruitment process and the music. Further damning evidence was that he had actually been in possession of four bottles of poison at the time of his arrest at Reading station. Also a letter was found on him addressed to the coroner via the police. In it he admitted poisoning his wife and it went on to outline his intention to return to Barn Cottage to give her a last kiss, murder baby Hollie and then kill himself. 'I should like our three bodies laid together,' he had written. On Monday 17th January 1921 the judge sentenced him to death. The fact that he had murdered his wife and intended Hollie to suffer the same fate was horrific enough but the trial revealed something else that sent shudders around the court and put into stark context the reason for his trespass into Miss Marks' room on the night of 29th September, which resulted in his assault on her.

On the afternoon of 29th September when Miss Marks was in Marlow waiting to return to the cottage, Mrs Bailey had been seen by a neighbour apparently in good spirits. She had indeed been the woman whom Lilian glimpsed through the doorway that morning whilst she was receiving tuition with Miss Field and Miss Edwards. Bailey had slipped stramonia in her tea that very afternoon and when she felt unwell because of this drug he had put her to bed in the back room where he fed her with prussic acid and, in a perverse attempt to ease the agony of that poison, gave her chloroform.

In answer to counsel's question, 'Where was your child then?', Bailey answered, 'In bed with my wife.'

The court was horrified as he went on to explain that he left his little girl next to her murdered mother and then had to concentrate on not letting Miss Marks enter that same room to comfort the crying child. That's why he insisted on entering her room and staying with her until the next morning.

When Miss Marks went downstairs to prepare the breakfast, he had bundled the corpse under the bed and brought Hollie downstairs, pretending she was his niece. That 3 year old child had spent 14 hours lying next to her murdered mother, and Miss Marks had spent the night with a murderer who attempted to rape her in a bedroom next door to his murder victim and his daughter.

Only a little over four months had passed since she answered that advertisement in the *Bucks Free Press* but things would never quite be the same again for Lilian Marks. That advert certainly did change her life.

Hollie was brought up by her grandmother in Devon and the subject of her real parents was a forbidden area of questioning. Her own imagination and snippets of overheard conversation led her to believe her parents had died in some sort of suicide pact. Three marriages and five children later, she began to seek the truth about her parents. Discovering she had been born in Winchester Prison, she also checked up on a vague memory about Oxford Prison and found her father had been executed there for murder in 1921. She obtained her mother's death certificate, which recorded death by poisoning.

So it was that, at the age of 66, she wrote to the *Bucks Free Press* asking them to help her find out the truth about that day in Little Marlow when she was only 3 years old. Robert Perrin, feature writer at the paper, listened to her story and together they visited Barn Cottage. Hollie recounted how she used to have recurring nightmares where she would be clawing at a mound of earth because she knew a body was underneath, but would stop before uncovering it. Now knowing the tragic reasons for that horrific dream, she was starting to understand the torment of her thoughts over the preceding years.

As for her father's claim to have invented 'the musical notation of the future', it had been dismissed in court as 'grossly grotesque, resembling a crude drawing of a trail of tadpoles seeking an incubator'. Bailey, however, passionately defended it to the end. After an unsuccessful appeal, George Arthur Bailey was executed on 2nd March 1921. His last words were to his High Wycombe solicitor, and they were: 'Don't let my music die.'

THE GUARDIAN OF CHAPEL COTTAGE

———————— ❁ ————————

Ghosts in popular myth are transparent, appear to float, possibly walk through walls and perhaps make strange noises. When tales of ghosts or apparitions are thoroughly investigated, and witnesses interviewed at length, a different picture emerges time and time again. Reliable informants rarely see semi-transparent beings, they have more usually been confronted by a solid, three-dimensional person. It then takes the brain a moment to register that there is something incongruous or out of place about what they are suddenly seeing, apart from why that person is there at all. The clothes are perhaps from another century, the whole appearance says this person is 'out of time'. Then they are gone, sometimes instantaneously, sometimes fading away. I began many such investigations as a sceptic, but the following experiences make it very difficult to do other than conclude that the the guardian of Chapel Cottage is as real as any ghost can be.

The story begins when a young married couple, Louise and Noel Dockstader, decided to move to the picturesque Buckinghamshire village of Speen. Noel originates from California and Louise from England and they had married and were living in California. Noel had an ambition to move to England and live in a historic house. Louise was keen to return to England and for Noel to experience English life away from what she called 'shiny, new California'. So, in 1991, after their first year of married life in the States, they rented a farm cottage in Gloucestershire and set about looking for a more permanent home.

They wanted an area with hills and countryside and close enough to travel to London for work and so their research took them to Speen. They took days out looking for 'For Sale' signs and in January 1992 came across Chapel Cottage.

No one was at home, so they peeked through the windows and both knew immediately that this was what they wanted. At that moment, the owners returned home from a walk and invited Louise and Noel in and sat them down by a roaring fire in the cottage's original 16th century inglenook fireplace. There was no question, this was their cottage.

By 22nd February 1992 they were driving down from Gloucestersire in a rented van to move into Chapel Cottage.

It was a mild February morning around 10 am when they arrived outside their new home. Their first job was to unload the many boxes they had managed to cram into the van, so they both got cracking and began carrying their possessions into the cottage. Noel was anxious to return to Gloucestershire for a second load whilst Louise sorted the first batch.

The cottage was even better than Louise remembered it.

As you opened the front door, you entered straight into a cosy living room and in the far left-hand corner there was a small stairwell from which steep, narrow polished wooden stairs spiralled upwards. They looked almost too vertical to climb safely and the stairwell entrance was enclosed by a small latched door. Louise thought they looked like stairs escaping from a small cupboard. Also you couldn't quite see where they were leading, which made them quite exciting. A major attraction of the cottage for Noel and Louise was not only this amazing staircase but all the nooks and crannies they could enjoy as well as the authentic inglenook fireplace that was almost half the size of the living room. It was an interesting design because it had an additional brick section right at the back halfway down that might have been there to throw heat forward into the room, or perhaps an unfinished attempt to open up the fireplace for the dining room behind. Anyway that was a puzzle to solve another day. They both loved the built-in bread oven and salt cupboard, all part of the original function of the fireplace when the early occupants would be busy cooking and baking bread over a log fire. They saw the possibilities of perhaps doing this again one day once they had settled in.

As they moved in on this February day in 1992, the first part of our story begins. Whilst Noel was busy unloading from the van, Louise was carrying the first box of possessions into the living room, and out of the corner of her eye she saw a figure standing on the stairs in the corner watching her. There is always a split second before the mind adjusts to what it has seen and Louise's immediate thought was, 'Oh the estate agent's here or someone Noel has asked to meet us but forgot to tell me.'

But no sooner had she thought this than she realised that the figure's appearance did not support her reasoning. The figure was male, completely solid – not the transparent apparition of the traditional ghost story – wearing a type of farm worker's smock and also a rather incongruous floppy hat over long curly black hair but it was difficult to see his face clearly. Louise's mind logged a similarity to how she would imagine Salvador Dali would look if you met him unexpectedly in your living room, but in an instant of recognition he had gone.

Louise recalls how she didn't scream; it seemed he was supposed to be there, the house was welcoming and there was no change in atmosphere or cold draught blowing across the small room as we think is supposed to happen if you see a ghost. Also it was mid-morning and in all good hauntings ghosts are not thought of as morning people.

Noel was called and, although not sceptical because Louise was certainly not prone to imaginary episodes, he kept an open mind that it was perhaps a strange configuration of the light or something that could be similarly explained.

However, during the course of that day while they moved in scores of packed boxes, both Louise and Noel did encounter a strange occurrence that neither has been able to account for, and that only happened on that first day in the empty cottage. They noticed something they have now called a 'reverse echo' precede them into the living room. As they carried in a box, the sound of footsteps went ahead of them as if someone invisible was already walking into the room. This was then accompanied by the sound of a box being thumped to the ground before the box Louise or Noel was carrying was placed down on the floorboards. It was as if their movements were being mimicked just ahead of them. As they both recall, 'It's like the sound was coming before the thing that you had done – in advance – and that was really spooky.'

That might have been the end of the very brief, bizarre experience they both found difficult to explain but something was yet to occur that Louise will never forget.

But first there were to be seven years of incredibly happy times in their cottage home without the slightest hint of ghostly happenings. In fact the house was one with a comforting atmosphere that soon put behind any lingering thoughts that it was haunted. Louise recalls how there was always a warm presence in the house; she described it as '... a wonderful house that had a really live feeling as if it was really taking care of us, and we hated to leave it but it was tiny'.

Before any question of leaving Chapel Cottage arises, however, there is the happy event of 1st July 1997 to record, the birth of their son, Joseph. Noel and Louise were overjoyed and Louise's mother came to stay at the cottage to help.

Noel, Louise and now Joe enjoyed two more happy years in Speen before deciding that it was time to move. The cottage was too small to bring up a family and the steep stairway and nooks and crannies were too tempting and possibly dangerous for a young toddler who was now a confirmed walker, zooming along with that toddling gait that youngsters use so effectively to reach quite remarkable speeds.

They settled on buying an old house with a large garden in nearby Prestwood, an ideal property to bring up a family and big enough to acquire a family dog as well.

The moving date was 10th July 1999 and Joe was now just over two years old and into everything. Eventually the cottage was cleared out ready for the new owners and was completely empty again, just as it had been when they moved in. Louise undertook a final check to make sure all was clean and tidy for the new occupants. She was carrying Joe in her arms back down the stairs after looking at the bedrooms and suddenly he made Louise stop and said, 'Mummy who's that?'

'Who?' Louise asked.

'That man', said Joe, 'with the funny clothes.'

'What man?'

'That man standing next to you, Mummy,' said Joe pointing.

Louise was halfway down the stairs holding Joe in front of her and anyone standing next to her would been in exactly the same spot where, seven years ago, Louise saw her ghost when she entered the living room of Chapel Cottage for the first time.

Five years before Joe was born.

Louise felt goose-bumps begin and, not daring to turn, she looked straight ahead and asked Joe what the man was doing.

'He's poking you, Mummy,' said Joe, demonstrating poking actions with his finger. Louise remembers how Joe was making eye contact with someone over her shoulder and even looked a little embarrassed at mimicking the stranger's actions.

Louise, now quite unnerved, plucked up the courage to whip around and confront the man but couldn't see anyone or anything. Joe, however, was looking straight at the spot where such a figure would be standing. Louise mumbled something about how they ought to go now; she didn't want to alarm Joe, and continued quickly down the stairs, went outside and locked the cottage door for the last time, never looking back.

Louise and Noel have thought about their ghost a great deal since and Louise in particular is frustrated about not knowing more about the house and its history. She also feels that perhaps the figure, or whatever it was, was only trying to communicate and now it is too late to find out why.

Joe doesn't talk about the incident as he has no reason to consider it as anything out of the ordinary. At two years of age he knew nothing of ghosts and wouldn't be worried about a man standing on the stairs, his finger prodding his mother. Noel and Louise did not discuss it with him either in case it frightened him.

Several things still puzzle Louise.

Chapel Cottage, Speen

Why did someone or something appear only when they moved in and then on the day they moved out, but in between the house felt so comforting and protective. Was this some kind of guardian? Did it watch over the family, thereby generating the warm presence that both Noel and Louise felt in their home? Also, why did she see him on their first day but only Joe could see him on their last day? And why would Joe say he was poking mummy?

Possibly because this is not what he really saw. It was likely that the apparition of Chapel Cottage wasn't poking at all, he was pointing.

But what on the stairs was he pointing at? It certainly wasn't Louise. Had he a story to tell? Did something happen on that staircase? From his position he could have been indicating the additional brick section that had been added after the original inglenook fireplace had been built.

Also, Joe had never prior to this incident, or since that day, claimed to have seen anyone who 'wasn't there' as far as mum or dad were concerned.

Louise recalls, rather chillingly, that the stairs were steep, rising up high into the roof space, and easily tall enough for someone to hang themself or be hung. But this would not accord with the friendly feel and happy atmosphere, so it seems more likely that attention was being drawn to something hidden in the area of the stairway.

The only other unusual event that Louise recalls happening during their time at Chapel Cottage – and this, on the face of it, seems totally unconnected with these two appearances of the Chapel Cottage ghost – concerns a visitor to the cottage.

It was 2nd July 1997, Noel had popped out for a short while and Louise was resting upstairs, having only just returned from Wycombe Hospital that very day with their one day old baby. It was Joe's very first time in his new home and Louise's mum had come to stay for while to help out. There was a knock at the cottage door and mum answered. It was an elderly stranger who introduced himself as someone who had been born in that cottage in 1900 and was back visiting the old village of Speen and his former home once more.

Louise could hear snatches of the conversation below as her mother chatted with him and he fully understood that it was not convenient to come in and look around whilst mother and new baby were resting. He thanked Louise's mother, who suggested he called back in a few days time.

For 97 years old, the visitor looked remarkably young.

A few days later a beautiful old photograph of Chapel Cottage was put through the letterbox with a brief note explaining that the young boy standing outside aged three years old was him in 1903.

He never called by again, unless ...

Was this a coincidence? Is there something that connects the unexpected caller on Joe's first day in the cottage with the apparition on the family's very first and very last day of occupation?

The mystery of the ghost of Chapel Cottage and the unexpected visitor remains to be solved.

A KWAKER ON THE TRAIN

❖

'What hath God wrought' (Samuel Morse 1844:
first telegraphic message from Washington to Baltimore)

The creation of Buckinghamshire in the 10th century established one of the smallest counties of England, at the same time altering many traditional land boundaries, most of them now forgotten. However, in more recent years, new boundary changes altered its territory once more. After ten centuries of Buckinghamshire history, in 1974, Slough and Eton were drawn into the adjoining county of Berkshire, the bureaucrat's pen in this case mightier than the warrior's sword of past battles. These boundary changes may also be forgotten one day but there are many tales of mystery and murder that belong to their original locations and cannot be taken away just by drawing a new line on a map.

A case in point is the extraordinary life and death of John Tawell. Truth can often be stranger than fiction and in this account of a Buckinghamshire murder we have a prime example. Here was a man who struggled for high social respectability and wealth and nearly made it against all the odds, but was so flawed as an individual, so selfish, callous and dangerous that he ended his life as a notorious murderer, entering the record books as the last person to be executed in front of County Hall in Aylesbury. He made the record books in other ways too, but these will be revealed as the story unfolds.

The tragic victim was his mistress, Sarah Hart, who lived at Salt Hill near Slough. It seems there was possibly another victim of Mr Tawell's murderous attentions – his first wife, but he literally got away with murder in her case, and might have done so again if it hadn't been for a concerned neighbour, a new invention and an undercover policeman.

Under a cloak of religious rectitude and social standing, John Tawell was far from the moral gentleman he professed to be. It would take some unravelling, however, for his real murderous nature to be revealed to the world and justice achieved for his crime against his mistress and mother of his children, Sarah Hart, on New Year's Day in 1845.

Before we reach that fateful day, and indeed enter old Buckinghamshire at all, there are certain things we need to know about our murderer.

John Tawell was born in 1784, a native of Aldeby in Norfolk. During his teenage years, he worked in a general stores for a widow who was a Quakeress. This religious group, known as the Society of Friends, fascinated Tawell and he made up his mind to become a Quaker. It was this ambition that was to fuel so much of what followed in his life.

The Society taught simplicity in all things and a particular respect for tolerance, justice and peace. It would become apparent during his later working life that John Tawell was intolerant of these principles – except the wish to be left in peace from those pursuing him for justice.

'Simplicity in all things' also evaded him as his life was to become more and more tangled and complicated. In his early 20s he began a job in London working for a large linen drapery business in Whitechapel. He had already formed a relationship with a woman from a Quaker family in Yarmouth and had applied for recognition as a Quaker. He was not accepted at first, but persevered and did receive the membership he craved by 24 years old. But it was short-lived. His sexual attentions to one of the housemaids working for his boss's family and her subsequent pregnancy put pressure on him to 'do the honourable thing', so he married her. She was not a Quakeress, and by 25 he was expelled from the Society of Friends for 'disorderly and unchaste conduct'. The disgrace of this rejection and his lifelong obsession to reverse it that would eventually take him as a 61 year old man on a bizarre, murderous journey to Salt Hill in Buckinghamshire.

Trapped in an unhappy marriage and with two children, Tawell changed his career. He became a travelling sales representative for a wholesale drug and patent medicine business in Queen Street, Cheapside. Now one of his close friends, Joseph Hunton from Yarmouth, was to lead him into a situation that would change the whole direction of his life and bring him into contact with Sarah Hart, his eventual victim.

Tawell's life-changing moment was his unmasking as a forger in 1814. In order to increase his wealth, and no doubt enjoy his times on the town with Joseph, he had taken up forgery and attempted to cash his home-made Bank of England cheque at the Uxbridge Bank of Hull and Co. Forgery was a capital offence, for which his friend would eventually be executed at Newgate in 1828, but John Tawell was in luck. He had picked on a Quaker bank for his crime, and because their religious principles did not allow them to support the taking of life, they did a deal. All he had to do was admit to uttering the cheque, but not to forging it in the first place. This would carry the lesser sentence of imprisonment for around seven years with hard labour.

Tawell pleaded guilty to the lesser charge but conducted his own legal case. When the inevitable guilty verdict was returned and before sentencing, he asked permission to address the court, which was granted. He made a long and eloquent speech asking that instead of imprisonment for seven years and the degradation that would bring, could the judge find it possible to transport him to Australia instead for period of fourteen years?

He'd rather have double the sentence in the New World than be in a London prison. He got his way and in 1814 was transported as a convict to that distant place on a fourteen-year sentence. And so began the remarkable 'stranger than fiction' turn around in his fortunes and his subsequent association with Sarah Hart. But first there would be seventeen years spent in Australia, the first four years or so working in the convict hospital in New South Wales, where his knowledge of patent medicines was put to good use. He made a favourable impression and with the assistance of the governor and friends amongst the colonial officials obtained an emancipation ticket. Within six years of setting foot in Australia, on 1st March 1820 he entered the record books for achieving the distinction of opening the first privately owned pharmacy, at 6, Hunter Street in Sydney. This became a very profitable business indeed. Estimates put his wealth at that time between £30,000 and £40,000.

His wife and children meanwhile, back in England, received no assistance at all until in 1824, ten years after his transportation, money was raised and a free passage granted for them to join him in Sydney. By now Tawell was having an affair with a local woman, so he was not too anxious to be reunited with his family.

He was wealthy, enjoying Australian life, moving in high society, and had a mistress. He didn't want his past back.

He had little choice, however, when his family arrived but after they had been in Australia for seven years, he decided to return to England with them in 1831, settling in Whitechapel once more. He continued to travel to Australia and back doing successful business deals.

Tawell was now in his mid 50s with wealth and status and all his ambitions achieved except one – to be accepted back by the Society of Friends. He had taken to dressing as Quaker at all times with greatcoat, broad brimmed hat and white cravat, but he needed official acceptance, real recognition. His wife and family were in the way of this. In 1838 he moved with his family to Bridge Street in Southwark where, unexpectedly, his wife was taken ill.

With his knowledge of drugs, Tawell attempted to treat her, but she started to deteriorate. It was at this time that he employed a domestic servant, 33 year old Sarah Hart, to help in the house and to nurse his wife. The medicine supplied by Tawell only made his wife worse and, despite Sarah's concerned care, she died. Sarah continued to work as Tawell's live-in domestic but became more than that, taking on the role of mistress of his house and giving birth to two children by him.

The status of a 36 year old unmarried mother in Victorian England was not to be envied. Inevitably it was the woman's morality that was questioned rather than that of the man who had fathered the children. Although Sarah didn't wear a wedding ring, she would tell friends about her husband, the Quaker who was once her master when she was in service. To keep up his image as a grieving and bereaved husband following the tragic death of his wife, Tawell moved Sarah out to accommodation at Crawford Street in Bryanston Square and then on to a small house next door to the King and Queen pub at Paddington Green and eventually out of sight of London society to Salt Hill, near Slough in Buckinghamshire. Even whilst Sarah was bearing his children he was having an affair with another Sarah, a Quaker widow called Sarah Cutforth, in Berkhamsted, in pursuit of his final ambition to be accepted back into the Quaker fold.

He certainly didn't want Sarah Hart as his wife when the opportunity presented itself, and he married Mrs Cutforth at a register office in Berkhamsted in 1841. He was seeking status and respectability within the Society of Friends, and Widow Cutforth was a respected Quakeress who kept a superior boarding school. The plan backfired when Mrs Cutforth, now Mrs Tawell, was excommunicated from the Society for marrying the disgraced John Tawell. This was a severe blow. Even worse was his constant fear of the discovery by his new Berkhamsted set that he was keeping a mistress and two children at Salt Hill near Slough in the adjoining county.

The year is 1845. Tawell is now 61, still dressing as a Quaker and unofficially accepted by the Berkhamsted Friends as such, living with his new wife, step-daughter and now a 15 month old baby son, in their sumptuous Hertfordshire home, called 'The Red House'. One son by his first marriage has died, the other son from that marriage has long since disappeared to make his way in the world. His mistress, Sarah Hart, now 40 years old, is living with her two illegitimate children, a boy and a girl, in a small cottage at Bath Place opposite the Castle Hotel in Salt Hill, Buckinghamshire. This consists of four small cottages owned by a friendly lady, Mrs Barrett. Sarah had told her that she was married and that her husband was the son of a Quaker gentleman named Tawell with whom she had formerly lived as a servant and he had gone abroad for five years or so.

Sarah was well liked by her neighbours living in the row of cottages at Salt Hill. She was poor and, with her two young children, surviving on an allowance from Tawell of £50 a year. Every three months, he would call at her cottage and give her twelve pounds, ten shillings to maintain herself and the children. He would stay briefly for a drink and a meal and then that would be last she and the children would see of him until another three months or so had passed. She did not talk to the neighbours about her husband visiting her as she continued to maintain he was abroad, but would say 'I expect my old master to visit', implying it was her husband's father bringing some of her husband's wages for the family's keep. This was no doubt a fiction composed by Tawell himself rather than Sarah, to safeguard his secret life. The neighbours were diplomatic about her plight, fully aware of her situation, but would not dream of speaking about it.

After Tawell's last visit at the end of September 1844, Sarah had become suddenly quite ill drinking Guinness with him. She had a

London friend, Charlotte Howard, staying with her, and whilst Charlotte had put her to bed to recover, Tawell had left thirteen sovereigns on the table and scuttled quietly away saying nothing. Charlotte came downstairs and with a fresh glass finished the rest of the bottle with no ill effects. Sarah shrugged her sickness off as being a result of something she'd eaten and regretted she had not been able to spend the evening as planned with Tawell, so she was especially looking forward to his New Year visit.

Around 2 pm on Wednesday 1st January 1845, Sarah's good neighbour Mrs Ashley called round for a chat. Sarah told her that she expected her 'old master' today, but it could be tomorrow. She said she was due some money from her husband and was in desperate need of it.

In the late afternoon, around 4.30 pm, Tawell arrived by train at Slough Station and made his way to the cottage to be greeted warmly by Sarah and his children. We do not know what excuse he would have made to Mrs Cutforth-Tawell, but she trusted him implicitly. His deceit, however, had been gnawing at him and he was fearful of revelation and more public humiliation, with him once again being labelled guilty of 'disorderly and unchaste conduct'.

His usual habit was to stay for dinner before parting with his twelve pounds, ten shillings. Around 6.15 pm he sent Sarah out to a nearby hotel called The Windmill to buy a bottle of Guinness stout. She asked the barmaid, Catherine White, if she could borrow a corkscrew and promised she would return it the next day. Sarah was in high spirits and on the way back to her cottage bumped into a local gardener, William Marlow. 'Ah Marlow,' she laughed. 'Oh Mrs Hart, what are you running for?' said Marlow. 'I've a visitor,' she replied, smiling, and ran on. It was now about 6.30 pm. What Sarah and Tawell talked about, how they got on, we do not know. The next thing we know about that evening was that about 7 pm Mrs Ashley, whose house was next door, was startled by a blood-curling scream coming from Sarah's cottage. She hurried out with a candle just in time to see Tawell struggling to open the garden gate. Asking what an earth was wrong, she managed to help him open it. Rather than answer, he hurried away towards Slough and a concerned Mrs Ashley rushed into the cottage.

There she found Sarah in her final death throes, writhing in agony on the floor, the children, thankfully, in bed upstairs.

Sarah's eyes were fixed, staring, but her lips were moving, and she made strange strangled noises.

'Oh Mrs Hart, what is the matter?' cried Mrs Ashley. Sarah didn't answer but squeezed her neighbour's hand. Mrs Ashley cradled her head and froth came from Sarah's mouth. Mrs Ashley noticed a bottle of stout on the table and two glasses, one empty and one half full.

She left Sarah and ran to the neighbouring cottages to summon help. Mrs Wheeler and Mrs Barrett came rushing in and they bathed Sarah's temples and threw vinegar in her face while one of Mrs Barrett's domestics ran to fetch Mr Champneys, a local surgeon who lived only 200 yards away. The doctor arrived within minutes and started to bleed her, but it was too late: Sarah Hart was dead.

Mrs Ashley told Mr Champneys about hearing Sarah scream and the man dressed as a Quaker rushing from the cottage towards Slough. She had seen him before, last September. Mr Champneys told Mrs Ashley to safeguard the bottle of stout and the tumblers and he set off in pursuit of Tawell.

Meanwhile Tawell had sped along, his long greatcoat flying as he made all haste towards Slough railway station. Local paper boy George Lewis knew Mr Tawell and when he saw him rushing towards him cried out, 'How are you Mr Tawell?'

Tawell didn't answer, but he looked up so there was no mistaking it was him. Reaching the station about 7.10 pm, Tawell saw an omnibus and hurrying up to the driver asked where he was heading. The driver told him Eton, so Tawell climbed aboard. 'Where do you want to get off?' asked the driver. 'Sir John Herschel's house,' was the reply. As this was only 400 yards away, it caused some surprise, but the bus set off and seconds later set him down outside this world famous astronomer's house in Slough.

Mr Weymouth, a local plasterer, was just going up to Herschel's house to meet up with his friend the butler there, when he saw John Tawell get off the bus, fiddle with his pocket until the bus departed and then set off on foot back to Slough Station. Whether he thought this would lay a false scent was never discovered. He then rushed into the railway station at around 7.32 pm and after speaking with Mr Howell, the Station Superintendent, about wanting to go to London, he was directed to the 7.42 train.

Mr Champneys arrived at the station just in time to see Tawell getting into a first class carriage for London. He quickly explained his suspicions to Mr Howell, but there was not enough time to authorise stopping the train, which set off for Paddington carrying a much relieved Tawell.

It is as this point in this extraordinary story that John Tawell enters the history and record books once more. Not as a murderer of Sarah Hart, because that was still to be discovered. Not for 'disorderly and unchaste conduct', or any other sins from his past, of which there were many, but for the means by which he was apprehended for questioning by the police. The new invention of the age was the five needle electric telegraph. Only recently communication lines had been opened up along railway routes, and Slough was one of those. A skilled operator could send upwards of 50 signals thousands of miles within a minute. It was decided that a message should be sent to Paddington Station by electric telegraph, alerting the police to follow Tawell so that they could judge the most appropriate moment of arrest for questioning about the untimely death of Sarah Hart.

The irony for Tawell was that as he sped towards London feeling more secure now that he had escaped Salt Hill, crucial information that would lead to his arrest was overtaking him electronically and would reach Paddington well before he did.

This was the first time police had used such a technique in pursuit of a suspect. One small drawback to this new communication system, however, was its inability to transmit the letters 'Q' or 'U'. So it was the following message that arrived at Paddington Station:

A MURDER HAS JUST BEEN COMMITTED AT SALT HILL AND THE SUSPECTED MURDERER WAS SEEN TO TAKE A FIRST CLASS TICKET TO LONDON BY THE TRAIN WHICH LEFT SLOUGH AT 7.42 PM. HE IS IN THE GARB OF A KWAKER WITH A GREAT COAT ON WHICH REACHES NEARLY DOWN TO HIS FEET. HE IS IN THE LAST COMPARTMENT OF THE SECOND FIRST CLASS COMPARTMENT.

The telegraphist at Paddington was somewhat confused by KWAKER, but realised after the same message was retransmitted

An advertisement for a telegraph demonstration to be held at Slough in 1839

twice more that he should substitute Q for K and U for W. The speed of transmission meant that the police had plenty of time to organise surveillance of Tawell. Police Sergeant William Williams of the Great Western Railway police covered his uniform with a coat and followed Tawell onto an omnibus, pretending to be a guard.

The telegraphic reply back to Slough read:

THE UP-TRAIN HAS ARRIVED, AND A PERSON ANSWERING IN EVERY RESPECT THE DESCRIPTION GIVEN BY THE TELEGRAPH CAME OUT OF THE COMPARTMENT MENTIONED. I POINTED THE MAN OUT TO SERGEANT WILLIAMS. THE MAN GOT INTO A NEW-ROAD OMNIBUS, AND SERGEANT WILLIAMS INTO THE SAME.

Tawell was tailed to Princess Street near the Bank, watched by Sergeant Williams who had concealed himself behind a statue. He was then tailed to the Jerusalem Coffee House, over London Bridge, to the Leopard Coffee Shop and then back to Cannon Street, then to a nearby lodging house at No. 7 Scott's Yard. Sergeant Williams waited about half an hour and then reported back to Mr Howell at Slough Station. For whatever reason, the police decided to do nothing until the following day when the Metropolitan Police were called in. However, when Inspector Wiggins from the Met and Sergeant Williams from the railway police called at the lodging house the following morning, Tawell had gone. It was fortunate that he was traced to the Jerusalem Coffee House around midday and questioned by the police. He was asked about his whereabouts on New Year's Day and whether he had travelled to Slough. He said he had been in London all that day and did not travel to Slough. He was then confronted with the evidence of his journey and the fact he was the chief suspect in a murder case. His reply is recorded as: 'You must be mistaken, my station in life must rebut any suspicions which might be attached to me.' On further questioning about the woman he was with last night, he said he knew no one in the vicinity of Slough, so could not have been at Sarah Hart's cottage. He said once more, 'Thee must be mistaken in the identity, my station in life places me beyond suspicion.'

The police knew otherwise and he was arrested on suspicion of the wilful murder of Sarah Hart of Salt Hill in Buckinghamshire and taken to the Three Tuns at Salt Hill, where the inquest was being held that very evening, Thursday 2nd January. At the inquest he was positively identified as the man visiting Sarah Hart on New Year's Day and taken into temporary police custody at the private home of Inspector Perkins, Inspector of Police for Eton, so he could appear at the continuation of the coroner's inquest the following Saturday, 4th January, and then again on Wednesday 8th January. Realising his inevitable exposure as Sarah's visitor, he claimed that she left his employment about five years previously and being a wilful person and he a kind person, she kept writing to him begging for money.

'She was a very good servant when in my service,' he went on, 'but was a very bad principled woman. She wrote that if I did not send her something she would make away with herself.'

He explained how he visited her and refused to give her any more money. She asked for stout and he sent out for some, which they shared. He then claimed she took out a small phial about the size of a thimble, poured it into her glass and drank it, throwing the remainder into the fire. She then 'done herself about' and laid on the floor. He thought she was bluffing, otherwise he would have got help, so he left. Asked if he had examples of the begging letters she was sending him, he said, 'No, I never keep such letters as those.'

After the inquest, he was remanded to Aylesbury for the March assizes there. Meanwhile, the inquest on poor Sarah revealed that she had died due to the consumption of a small amount of prussic acid. The police suspected that Tawell had poisoned her glass of stout during his visit on New Year's Day. Now they had to prove it. There was no evidence of a glass phial thrown into the fire as he had claimed. But after a detailed search they did locate a small phial in a cupboard and then two more inside a jug but they revealed little useful information. More valuable was the evidence of the assistant to Mr Hughes the chemist of 89, Bishopsgate Street-within, who was taken down to Aylesbury Gaol, where he positively identified Tawell as someone buying prussic acid on the day of the murder.

Despite this undeniable identification, Tawell was confident that he would be acquitted and he was supported by his

Berkhamsted friends. His wife stood by him, protesting that the whole situation was a lie and her husband was an innocent man caught up in a nightmare he knew nothing about. The prussic acid was merely his personal treatment for varicose veins.

The three day trial was a sensational one, which took a very unexpected turn that was based on claims about the nature of the common apple. It began on 12th March 1845 before Mr Baron Park (later to become Lord Wensleydale), and the prosecution's case was damning. They detailed Tawell's extra-marital relationship with Sarah Hart and showed that it had been an affair of long standing. They could also establish his extensive knowledge of drugs and medicines, given his long and successful career in that field. They then were able to reveal the finding of a bottle of Steel's Acid in his possession. This patent treatment for varicose veins contained prussic acid. They proved he had purchased two bottles from Mr Hughes' chemist's shop. One was bought on Wednesday 1st January, the day of the murder. Then, he had gone back to the chemist just prior to his arrest at the Coffee House claiming he'd lost the bottle he bought the previous day and so purchased another. Evidence was also given by Charlotte Howard about the previous September, when Sarah had become suddenly quite ill drinking Guinness with him, yet Charlotte had finished the bottle in a clean glass with no ill effects. Was this intended to be Sarah's day to be murdered but somehow he had failed and Sarah had survived?

When it was time for the defence council, Mr Fitzroy Kelly, QC (later to become Chief Baron of the Exchequer), to speak the court was hushed. He looked at the jury and said one word, 'Applepips.'

He then went to great pains to point out to the jury that a natural source of prussic acid was applepips. 'In no other substance in nature, excepting bitter almonds, do you find such a concentration of the poison.'

The post-mortem on Sarah Hart had revealed a quantity of applepips in her stomach. In fact, that Christmas it was claimed she had been given a present of a sack of apples and had eaten very many into the New Year. Sarah, he claimed, had died from eating applepips and his client was innocent, merely the possessor of a common treatment for varicose veins, which he used on himself. Also there had been no smell of prussic acid in the victim's throat or in the room. A faint trace only was found in her intestines.

It was 6 pm on the second day of the trial and the defence's claim was sensational. It was also a bad day for apple-growers and local fruit markets, who were soon to become victims of a widespread apple scare. An apple a day was supposed to keep the doctor away, not the other way around. The trial could now go either way, and Tawell was so confident that he had a carriage waiting outside the White Hart Inn at Aylesbury ready for his acquittal. Many wagers were made on the trial's outcome.

From then onwards, Mr Fitzroy Kelly became a 'media star' known as 'Applepip Kelly'.

On the final day of the trial the judge was less impressed than many in the court about the claim that Sarah had inadvertently killed herself by eating too many apples. His summing up put this unlikely explanation into the total context of the prosecution's evidence and the strong motive Tawell had for ridding himself of his mistress. The prosecution had delivered a convincing case against John Tawell and he had denied going to Slough on the day of the murder and also professed to not knowing anyone living at Salt Hill. He was a proven liar.

The jury took 30 minutes to return a verdict of 'Guilty'. The court was stunned into silence. The judge then put on the black cap and pronounced the sentence of death.

A Mr J.K. Fowler, who was responsible for accompanying Mrs Tawell (the former Mrs Cutforth) to visit her condemned husband at Aylesbury Gaol, described this final visit as follows: 'After his condemnation his poor suffering wife came to visit him, and I escorted her to see her husband. I shall never forget her sorrow and heart-broken grief, nor the appearance of the wretched man. As I entered the parlour of the governor's house, where the interview was to take place, he came in with his warder through another door. He seemed completely paralyzed at the sight of his wife, and turned deadly pale; a poor, insignificant little man in his Quaker's garb, looking utterly miserable.'

At dawn on Friday 28th March, a cold, windy morning with snow on the ground, four men worked tirelessly on constructing the gallows outside County Hall in Aylesbury. Tawell would have heard the sounds of their grim construction work from his cell. Whilst they toiled in the early light, spectators had already begun to arrive in Market Square to secure the best views. From around 6 am, the crowds really started to gather and by 7.30 am upwards of six thousand people were crammed into the square. Many were women who had been avidly following the trial of this cheating husband and self-proclaimed Friend. Driving sleet buffeted their faces as they strained to see the final moments of John Tawell, the counterfeit Quaker, who had callously and calculatedly poisoned his mistress and mother of his children, Sarah Hart.

Around 7.40 am, Tawell was brought towards the balcony of County Hall and led up the five steps to the scaffold. The familiar figure of Calcraft, the hangman, placed the black cap over his head. Tawell asked for time to pray. He knelt briefly, then stood as the rope was adjusted around his neck, thrown swiftly over the beam and tied with three half hitches.

There was a brief moment of tangible energy emanating from the vast crowd, whose collective thoughts came to the forefront as each individual, speaking quietly to themselves, realised they were speaking in unity, and out loud. As if rehearsed, the words 'now … now' ran around the spectators, willing Calcraft to pull the bolts to open the drop.

Bang, and at 7.45 am, the trap opened and Tawell dropped like a stone.

Mr Fowler, the same observer who had witnessed his final meeting with his wife, had this to say about Tawall's last moments of life: 'When the bolt was drawn, the wind so buffeted about the wretched little body of the murderer, that it was believed by many he was struggling still for half an hour afterwards. Calcraft, the executioner, however, declared that the man died instantly.'

The crowd had got their result earlier than scheduled and those only just arriving for an 8 am hanging cursed Calcraft for spoiling their sport. All they had was a swaying corpse to watch for the next hour until Tawell was cut down at a quarter to nine and taken away for a 10 am burial in unconsecrated ground – the final insult to his ambitions.

We must not forget that, compared to Tawell, his tragic victim Sarah Hart had died in agony. His two illegitimate children by that affair were taken into care by the parishes in which they were born, one to Marylebone, the other to Chiswick. Also, Tawell's first wife had died after a long illness that was never satisfactorily explained but poison of some kind was now suspected, though it can never be proved.

He also leaves behind a mystery about his real feelings, emotions and motives for what happened in that small cottage at Salt Hill. His confession to Reverend Cox, the Chaplain at Aylesbury Gaol, was never revealed to the County Justices. They put immense pressure on Revd Cox, who would not relate what he had been told. On 2nd May, the Duke of Buckingham bought this issue of Revd Cox's refusal to release Tawell's confession before the House of Lords. Cox was severely criticised for not co-operating and was forced to leave his post as gaol chaplain. He never did relent and we will never know the full story and inner emotions that John Tawell confessed to his priest before that final cold March day outside Buckinghamshire's County Hall.

THE TRAGEDY OF
ALICE TURNEY

---❁---

Women do not feature amongst murderers in any significant numbers.
Whatever the year or era examined, women are less likely to murder than their male counterparts and we can take some comfort from that. The reasons why this should be so are not clear. Many feel that women have greater self discipline and regard for human life as it is they who give birth to it in the first place.

Consequently, one of the most tragic of murderous acts is that of a mother who murders her child. Seeking an explanation or understanding of such a horrendous deed is a difficult quest. It is an act that tears at the observer's emotions both for the mother so desperately brought to do such a thing, and for the innocent victim.

Such a case in recent Buckinghamshire history is that of Alice Rose Turney from Tinkers End in Winslow, in 1923. At the age of 20, Alice, like many young women in the 1920s, was working away from home in domestic service. In fact she left home at fourteen years of age to earn her own living and to help support her Winslow family, whom she visited as often as possible.

For Alice, a romantic liaison with a young man in the autumn of 1922 led to one of the worst situations that could confront a young working woman of that era. She was carrying his baby and was unmarried.

We do not know what anguish Alice suffered wondering what to do when it was clear the father had no intention of marrying her. Many young women submitted themselves to the extreme perils of back-street abortionists, or perhaps sought dangerous remedies from local women who knew about these things but were never spoken of until desperate measures were necessary. Some girls in such circumstances were even hidden away in mental institutions whilst others were conveniently forgotten by their families. Social etiquette, an upstanding moral appearance and fear of embarrassment had a high price in some quarters.

Alice, however, was a working woman, not dependent on her Winslow parents, and made her own decision to have her baby.

Edward John Turney was born on 25th June 1923 in the Cottage Hospital at Willesden, London, close to where Alice was working at Wembley. It was testament to her employers at that time that she was able to return to work after Edward's birth and take up her duties again. Whether a condition was the fostering out and, later, the adoption of her baby is not clear, but we know that the Willesden Board of Guardians soon made arrangements for Edward Turney to be fostered.

Mrs May Elizabeth Birch, a widow of 9, Holly-lane, Harlesdon, took over the care of baby Edward on 10th July when he was three weeks old. This meant that Alice's time was now split between her domestic work in Wembley, going to see her baby at Mrs Birch's house in Harlesden and visiting her mother at Tinkers End in Winslow, Bucks.

Unfortunately in March of that same year, Alice's father had been committed by Dr Leapingwell, a local Winslow doctor, to the Bucks County Medical Hospital at Stone, where he had been classified as a lunatic, so her mother appreciated her daughter's visits very much. The double stigma of having an illegitimate grandson and a husband in a mental institution made small village life difficult for her and Alice's sister Catherine. Alice, on the other hand, could always escape from the gossips of Winslow to the anonymity of the London suburbs.

It had also been in March of that year, when Alice was five months pregnant, that the father of her baby denied it was his and would have nothing more to do with her. It is a tribute to Alice's determination that her baby should be cared for properly that, on 11th August, she took out a summons against him to pay maintenance. He failed to turn up at Wealdstone Court and in his absence was ordered to give Alice 10 shillings a week, which he never did.

Alice Turney loved her baby and went to visit him every week, sometimes twice a week, and she made sure that she always handed over enough money for his keep. She had told Mrs Birch that Edward was a delicate baby and needed lots of care.

Mrs Birch made sure he was taken regularly to the Willesden clinic. Towards the end of September, however, the child had been reported as having fits, so the doctor at the clinic advised a visit to the cottage hospital. Alice had also been devastated by the news that her father had died in Stone Asylum that same month.

Mrs Birch telegraphed Alice, who rushed round the following morning and signed the papers for her baby to be admitted to hospital. Edward spent two weeks there, visited regularly by Alice, and, although he was still very thin, she happily brought him back to the care of Mrs Birch, where he grew stronger and thrived.

Alice would make the journey to Winslow Road Station and Tinkers End to visit her widowed mother as often as she could after her father died, and would tell her mother about how well Edward was doing and how one day perhaps she would be able to have him back. She might even get permission to bring him to see his grandmother at Winslow.

Edward was soon to make a trip with his mother to Winslow but it was one of such great tragedy and horror that it is difficult to fully comprehend, particularly when it seemed Alice had come through the worst part of being an unmarried mother in those morally censorious times.

It began with a postcard sent by Alice to Mrs Birch on 23rd October. Edward was now four months old and doing well under his foster-mother's care supplemented by his mother's loving visits. The card said:

> Dear Mrs Birch, I am sorry to give you such short notice, but my mother knows of a lady who has offered to take baby and bring it up as her own. Do not bother about clothes, I will call for them some other time.

On that same day, around 11 am, Alice called to collect her baby. Mrs Birch said to her, 'Alice, do you know this lady baby is going to?' Alice replied, 'No, Mrs Birch, but my mother does.'

Mrs Birch thought it must be in Winslow, but Alice said the lady who was going to adopt Edward lived in Purley, Surrey and that's all she knew. She needed to see her mother in Winslow to find out more. Mrs Birch was concerned about what would happen if this lady decided not to adopt the baby. Alice said she did not know what she would do if the lady did not go ahead with the adoption.

Mrs Birch said she would gladly take Edward back and perhaps he could then go into the foundling hospital if that would help find him a new home.

Alice agreed and said, 'Very well Mrs Birch, we will arrange that if I am not back by six o'clock tonight with baby, you will know that everything is settled.'

In view of what was soon to occur, Alice's last words to Mrs Birch have a chilling resonance to them.

She took Edward warmly dressed with two vests, a woolly pale blue coat and wrapped in a white shawl. Alice promised to keep in touch.

Mrs Birch heard nothing so wrote to Alice the next day to learn more about Edward's new family in Surrey. She received a reply by return of post which read:

Dear Mrs Birch,

I like the look of Mrs Smith very much. She is very pleased with baby. She has already got a cot for it to sleep in and a pram to take it out in. She has a lovely house and the lady is kindness itself. She gave me ten shillings to get myself something to eat. Will you get ready two bedgowns and four napkins, and I will come over for them on Wednesday: Sunday if possible. All the other clothes you have.

Alice Turney

Alice never called.

True to her word, Alice did visit her mother in Winslow on the day she took her baby back from Mrs Birch. It was a brief visit from about 4.30 pm, leaving in time to catch the 6 pm train from Winslow Road Station to Harrow-on-the-Hill and thence by bus to Harrow Weald and a train to Wembley, finally walking to her employers' house.

Edward, however, was not with her, nor with any Mrs Smith in Surrey, and he had still not met his grandmother who had no reason to assume other than he was warm and safe with Mrs Birch. Alice had told her she had been to Aylesbury on business and was just popping by before going home to Wembley.

So what did happen on 23rd October 1923 and where was Edward John Turney?

The tragic truth would not be known for another ten days when, at approximately 8 pm on 2nd November, Alice went up to a police constable in Croydon and said, 'I want you to have me up for the wilful murder of my child.'

PC Sidney Bean took her to Croydon police station, where she explained that she wished to tell him all about it and get it off her mind. At 8.30 pm that day she made a statement to Detective Inspector Hedges that, even as an experienced police officer, he found difficult to fully comprehend. The truth about Edward was eventually to be found in Winslow, Buckinghamshire.

Alice's statement detailing what had happened when she left Mrs Birch's house with Edward was as follows:

'I took the child straight to 19, Raneleigh Road, Wembley as my mistress was away from home all day. I arrived there at 11.50 am. At 12 o'clock I took the child to my bedroom at the top of the house and tied a piece of towel round its neck and stuffed a small handkerchief in its mouth. I waited until the child died, and then pulled the handkerchief a little way out of its mouth and then lit the handkerchief to try and discolour the face. The handkerchief would not burn very well, so I put the child just as it was, with all its clothes on, with the handkerchief in its mouth and the cloth round its neck, into my dressing-case. I left the house with the child in the dressing-case and took the train from Wembley Road Station to Harrow Weald. I took a 'bus from there to Harrow-on-the-Hill and caught the two o'clock train for Winslow Road Station. I arrived there just after 4 pm. After leaving the station, I carried the child in my dressing-case down the road to the brook, which is about three minutes' walk.

I entered the field of Monk's Farm in the Claydon Road and about three or four yards from the bridge, I threw the dead body into the water.

I then got onto the main road again, and went straight home to see my mother, and told her I had been to Aylesbury on business. I caught the 6 o'clock train back from Winslow Road Station and went straight to my situation and I have not been to Winslow since.'

On Monday 5th November a pale and distressed Mrs May Elizabeth Birch confirmed the terrible truth and in the presence of the coroner at Winslow police station, identified the swollen, burnt and bruised body recovered from Claydon Brook the day

Claydon Brook, Winslow, where Alice disposed of the body

before, as that of baby Edward Turney, aged four months. Alice, who had by now been charged with the wilful murder of her child, had declined her right to attend the inquest and was in custody at Holloway Prison.

Edward was discovered just as Alice had said. The pathetic little body was clothed and found in 4 ft deep water at about the same distance from the bank. A piece of towelling was tied tightly around his neck, as Alice had recounted, and a bit of partly burnt linen wedged into his mouth. This terrible discovery was recorded as being 240 yards from Winslow Road Station and just over a mile from Alice's family home at Tinkers End.

When Dr Leapingwell examined Edward, he noted how the head, face and hands were covered with thick slime from the body's time in the water. When he removed the cloth from the baby's mouth, his tongue had been doubled back on itself. There were also burns on the right side of both lips and the first finger of the right hand was also burnt. There was another burn on the left knee but no other signs of violence.

The coroner, Mr G.H.M. Barker, also heard from Doris Alice Putnam of 1, Western Lane, Winslow, who confirmed seeing Alice

Rose Turney in Winslow on the day Edward was taken from Mrs Birch's care.

Mr Barker concluded that Alice, haunted by her terrible secret and remorse, had been driven to confess. What she had said had now been confirmed by the tragic discovery in Claydon Brook, Winslow, so the verdict had to be that of the wilful murder of Edward John Turney by Alice Rose Turney. The relatively new offence of infanticide could not apply as Edward was four months old at the time of his death and not a newly born baby in the care of a clearly distressed and mentally distraught mother, as happens from time to time.

As directed by the coroner, the jury returned a verdict of wilful murder against Alice Rose Turney.

At the Old Bailey Central Criminal Court on Thursday 6th December 1923, Alice, aged 20, described in court as an unmarried domestic servant, was found guilty of the murder of her four month old son and sentenced to death. Alice had pleaded not guilty. Her defence had claimed she was insane at the time of this wilful act.

The jury had taken this possibility into account and, whilst returning a guilty verdict, did make a strong recommendation to mercy before Mr Justice Avory passed sentence of death upon her.

Evidence had been given by Dr Morton, Governor of Holloway Prison, that Alice had the mental intelligence of a girl between eleven and twelve years of age and, although sane in legal terms, was in his opinion mentally deficient.

This, however, is not the end of the tragic story of Alice Rose Turney from Winslow.

We will never know the full impact that the committal of her father to Stone Asylum and his classification, in the stark terminology of the time, as a lunatic had upon her. Also he died in Stone just at the time that her own baby was reported as having fits. Dr Leapingwell, who attended the Turney family in Winslow, also confirmed in evidence that he had certified as insane one of her aunts and he knew of an uncle who had also been committed to Stone Asylum.

Did Alice harbour a secret fear of inherited insanity and felt she was saving Edward from such a fate? Our contemporary knowledge of post-natal depression would also offer up other persuasive medical explanations not available to juries at that time.

Alice was not executed. The Home Secretary listened to the recommendation for mercy and commuted the death sentence. She went back to Buckinghamshire once more, but this time to Stone Asylum rather than Tinkers End, having to live with the terrible nightmare of that day, 23rd October 1923, when her baby came with her to Winslow. How could Mrs Birch, or anyone, have realised the real meaning of Alice's last words to her before she took Edward away for the last time:

'If I am not back by six o'clock tonight with baby, you will know that everything is settled.'

BUCKS BEASTS AND THE GHOST DOG OF TINGEWICK

————— ❀ —————

Superstitions and legends abound when it comes to animal ghosts and their meanings. Buckinghamshire, like many other counties, has had many independent sightings reported of big cat or puma type animals roaming the countryside. The so-called 'Beast of Bucks' was seen as recently as March 2003 by staff at a furniture manufacturers in Princes Risborough, one witness describing it as '… jet black and much bigger than a cat'. Golfers at Wycombe Heights reported the same in May 2001 and puma-like tracks were discovered nearby. It was the report of a large cat-like creature in Stoke Poges on 12th November 1964 by two policemen that began this Buckinghamshire legend, reinforced when there were several sightings of a big cat-like creature at Stokenchurch in 1983. In fact, when the chronologies of 'big cat/beast' sightings are compared across counties from Buckinghamshire to Derbyshire to Devon, most are reported in 1983. Also, the sightings cluster around the same months, February through to June. Of the isolated incidents that have been reported before and since nothing matches the 1983 sightings, particularly in Buckinghamshire. Is there a mystery connection yet to be discovered about that year?

Dogs, particularly large black dogs, are one of the most frequently reported ghostly animals. Because of the high frequency of such reports, many researchers treat their occurrence as a phenomenon in its own right. The origin of ghostly dog sightings goes back to legend and superstition at a time when new graveyards were begun. No one wanted to be the first to be buried in a new graveyard, or at least their family would not want it for them. Superstition held that the first-buried would have to take on the duty of guardian to all the other souls that followed. For eternity their role was to guard the graveyard. To avoid this happening, a dog, usually a large black dog, was killed and buried as the first soul in the graveyard. It would then have to take on the duty of guarding the human occupants that followed.

Such a dog would, on occasions, be said to come to the rescue of the living if they were in danger of attack or other perils within the territory of the guardian. So, alongside big cat or beast sightings, the reports are also littered with big black dog sightings, usually near churchyards.

The most significant, strange and unexplained mysteries associated with dogs are reports that people make of seeing a dog just before someone's death. For example, someone sees a dog they recognise as belonging to a friend or relative but it appears unexpectedly and briefly in their house and then fades away. The person seeing the dog calls up their friend to relate the story only to learn that their friend had died at approximately the same time the vision of the dog appeared.

My only experience of a related phenomenon, also associated with the vision of a dog, was a telephone call from my mother ringing to tell me she had been woken up by Gina, the family Airedale, sitting on her bed but then disappearing. The only problem was that my mother lived in Stoke Poges in Bucks, I was living in Hillingdon and Gina the Airedale, who actually belonged to my in-laws, had retired to Malta with them some years previously. She was worried the dog had somehow found its way back to Stoke Poges, where it had stayed quite often in the past, and she didn't know what to think. Logic told her it was impossible to believe Gina had found her way to her house, but she was there briefly, and very clearly. Although late at night, I telephoned Malta only to discover that Gina had died at the same time my mother had seen her appear in her bedroom and my in-laws were anxiously debating how they were going to break the news to their daughter and me.

It seems from reports of this kind that either the vision that appears has just died, as in the case of Gina, or someone associated with that vision is in trouble and possibly dying. What are known by ghost experts as 'ghosts of the living' generally appear once only and often from locations far away. The person seeing the ghost is normally alerted to contact that person, who is often near death or has in fact died by the time the contact is made. Modern theories about his phenomenon now refer to situations where extreme danger can trigger telepathic thought signals. The receiver of these powerful signals admits them straight into their brain, which has tuned in without the person even thinking. They are taken totally by surprise. The brain then converts the signals it receives to a recognisable picture for the eye, which is then seen as a real image. Twin studies will often reveal unexpected telepathic connections when one of the twins is in difficulty. These are also known as 'crisis apparitions'. So either the person or animal is sending an image of themselves or a 'messenger' on their behalf, typically a dog, to visit close friends or relatives

It is very rare indeed to come across a big cat, beast or ghost dog that has been photographed, but this is what happened in the small Buckinghamshire village of Tingewick in 1916, the so-called 'Ghost Dog of Tingewick'.

The story begins with a man called Arthur Augustus Springer. From a hectic 25 years serving in the Metropolitan Police he had retired as a high ranking CID officer in 1915. He'd had enough of city life and retreated to the rural calm of Tingewick. By the time

The ghost dog photographed at Tingewick c.1916 by Arthur Springer, retired CID Inspector. (© Fortean Picture Library)

he was settled it was two years into the Great War, and, had he been a younger man, as he never failed to tell anyone who would listen, he'd have signed up like a shot. As it was, he'd done his bit catching villains, and was now enjoying his well-earned retirement. A keen photographer, he spent a lot of time capturing images of this picturesque area of north Bucks, but there was one photographic occasion that was to lead Arthur into one of the most famous mysteries associated with ghostly animal sightings.

One fine, warm summer's day Arthur was invited to take tea with two ladies in the village. As usual, he had his camera with him to record the occasion. He took a series of photographs of the scene and enjoyed a pleasant afternoon's conversation over tea and home-made cakes.

A few days later, when he called by to pass the time of day, the maid told him that the lady of the house had been called away the very evening of the tea party to her sister, who had suddenly been taken very ill and was not expected to recover. It was a few days later again, when Arthur had the photos of that afternoon developed and the puzzle began.

In one photograph there was an undeniable, but ghostly image of a dog with an indistinct head, standing next to the lady who had been summoned that very day to her sick sister. No dog lived at the Tingewick house and Arthur had not taken a photograph of a dog elsewhere that could have created a double exposure. The negatives were found to be quite normal on either side of this particular frame. The dog appeared at that precise moment on that summer's day to be captured by Arthur's camera. No one, however, had noticed a dog in the garden or knew whose dog it was – until the lady who had been called away saw the picture. It was very much like her sister's dog. Was this a warning image that did not succeed in becoming fully formed and so was unable to arouse the attention of the lady concerned? Its headless appearance could suggest that the telepathic signals were not strong enough to enable it to succeed as a messenger from her sister, who died shortly afterwards.

Dismissed by some as a hoax and others as an innocent double exposure, Arthur Springer's 'Ghost Dog of Tingewick' photograph could be a unique glimpse of a genuine 'crisis apparition'.

BUCKINGHAMSHIRE'S VERY LAST PUBLIC EXECUTION

———————❁———————

'Thine icy heart I well can bear,
But not the love that others share.'
(Eleanor Anne Franklin, 'Coeur de Lion', 1822)

Unrequited love can be a powerful trigger that pushes the pursuer beyond reason to a tragic ending for themselves as well as the object of their desire. For William Stevens, a young man of 25, his emotional turmoil at being in love with young 17 year old Annie Leeson, who would not acknowledge his affection, became unbearable.

She literally was, the girl next door, in the shire town of Buckingham. The year is 1864.

William had already completed a successful apprenticeship to become a tailor and had worked in London for over two years but wanted to return home to establish his new trade in his home town of Buckingham. He moved in with his parents, who lived in the same cottage tenement as Widow Leeson, whose two youngest daughters were Annie and Elizabeth.

Annie was not living with her mother and elder sister but had accommodation as a domestic servant, working for Mr James Uff, the local butcher and grocer.

This was no distance away and she visited her family as often as possible, so she remained as good as 'the girl next door' whom William wanted for his own. Annie was very beautiful, quite tall with bright dark eyes, a fine rosy complexion and a mass of tumbling dark hair. She was always laughing and joking and the local lads admired her greatly.

William would speak with her as often as possible and early in 1864 he planned to try and win her over with Valentine cards. But 14th February came and went and Annie did not succumb to his

Valentine wishes. In fact William became angry over an offensive Valentine he had received and called to speak to Mr Uff, who he was told knew something about it. Mr Uff said he had no knowledge of such a Valentine or who sent it and Annie denied it was her. William told Annie that if she were ever to marry someone else he would blow his brains out.

Was this the trigger that began his pathological concerns that others were getting Annie's love when it should be him? He was certainly depressed at work, as his colleague John Billing had been observing. John and William would go for a couple of pints in the Bell or sometimes the Barrel and he would speak of his love for Annie and how hard life was treating him.

He also took to carrying a razor, which alarmed his father, Robert Stevens, who attempted to dissuade him. William, however, became submerged in his tortuous thoughts of rejection by the girl he loved and even muttered to work colleague John that it was only the law that was holding him back. At the time, this didn't make any sense, so John let it pass.

Annie's relationship with William was described by her sister Elizabeth as 'on and off'. It seemed to be finally 'off' on Sunday evening, 21st February, when a very angry Annie came into her mother's house whilst she and Elizabeth were eating supper. Annie said that William had behaved improperly towards her and she would not walk with him again.

When Annie went to visit another sister living nearby in Well Street that Thursday, she wanted Elizabeth to go with her but Elizabeth wasn't feeling too well, so she went on her own and William followed her and waited outside but did not bother her.

As with most behaviours that begin to border on pathological or manic depressive, observers only saw one small part of what would become a complex jigsaw puzzle that William Stevens was piecing together inside his head. John Billing knew he was depressed and heard him saying that he'd cut Annie's throat if she didn't return his affections. Elizabeth was aware that he had a razor on him and Annie herself had been shown the razor by William. Perhaps this was in an emotional plea that he might kill himself if she did not return his love or had he threatened to kill her to her face?

We will never know because tragic events rapidly took over that could never be undone.

About 6 pm on Saturday 27th February, Annie finished work and called round to her mother's house where she found Elizabeth sitting alone in the front room. No sooner had Annie arrived than they both heard footsteps in the outside passageway leading to the back kitchen. They knew it was William. Annie waited and said, 'Lizzie, he's gone down the yard, I'll go now.' Annie set off to fetch some water from the pump at the corner of the churchyard to take back to her lodgings at Mr Uff's.

Meanwhile William had gone upstairs to his room and was getting ready to go out for the evening, possibly to drown his sorrows with John at the Barrel. What was going on in William's head must have been a tumult of confusion, because, on glancing out of the window and seeing her go past to fetch water from the pump, something snapped and he dashed down the stairs.

Young Richard Woolhead, aged eleven, was witness to the next terrible scene. He was coming up by the churchyard, where the pump stood, and saw Annie fill her bucket. He was interested in some boys playing at tops and was walking behind Annie as she went back to her mother's house and set the full bucket down outside the door. Annie went in the house and about four or five minutes passed before she emerged, picked up the bucket and set off towards Mr Uff's. It was then that William Stevens rushed past and caught up with her on the corner of Tingewick Road opposite Mill Corner.

After a brief confrontation, Annie tried to run but he grabbed her in the crook of his arm. Taking out the cut-throat razor he had been carrying, that is exactly what he used it for. He drew the razor into her neck with an immense and terrible force.

In that brief moment of frozen time, Annie managed to scream 'murder' and run with her head lolling, blood cascading down her dress as she struggled into Mr Uff's shop. Her employer, who was serving a customer, rushed from behind the counter and caught her in his arms, Annie's life-blood drenching his apron. He quickly carried her into the back house, calling frantically for a cloth to stem the bleeding, but it was too late. Annie died in his arms as he tried to assist her. He was distraught with grief.

Local police constable Richard Seaton was witness to the final scene in Annie's life. He had been present in the shop as the fatally injured young girl collapsed into Mr Uff's arms. He immediately went to get medical assistance in the shape of local doctor Dr De'ath.

Meanwhile, the frenzied William had run home. The tragedy in his head had become reality, acted out by his own hand. No other was to share Annie's love if he could not do so. Elizabeth, unaware of the appalling attack on her sister, was startled by a noise outside as if someone had fallen down. Her immediate thought was that Stevens had grabbed hold of Annie in the passageway, so she leapt to the door and went out.

There lying on the stones was William Stevens, bleeding from cuts to his throat, a black-handled razor in his bloodstained hand. She screamed, and William's mother came to see what had happened and distraught ran into the street shouting, 'My son has cut his throat.' Widow Leeson ran to Mr Uff's for help only to discover that her daughter lay dead, murdered, her windpipe, gullet and vessels of her neck cut through.

Dr De'ath arrived at Mr Uff's but on being told Annie was dead, did not go in, rushing instead to check on Stevens in case he was

This street leading to the Tingewick road is where, in 1864, young Richard Woolhead saw the murder take place

alive. He found him lying in the passage and bleeding profusely from the throat. Other residents had come rushing into the street as a result of the pandemonium, screaming and shouting. Stevens was still alive, and his mother in hysterics as she picked up the razor by her son's side.

The doctor and others carried Stevens into the house, where he washed the wound, quickly sewing up the gash to his throat. Satisfied he could do no more, the doctor went back to Mr Uff's to examine the murdered girl.

The town was in a turmoil as the rumour spread rapidly that William Stevens had murdered Annie Leeson and committed suicide after his vicious attack on his would-be sweetheart.

Tragic Annie Leeson was left, as she had died, on the floor of Mr Uff's house, awaiting the visit of the coroner and jury to the crime scene the following day.

It was, of course, a murder without the complications of seeking witnesses, motive, weapon or murderer. All were known.

Dr De'ath may have been unable to save poor Annie, but Steven's suicide bid seemed to have failed; he did not die that day as expected but hung precariously onto life. The families were grief-stricken. When the coroner and his jury held the inquest on Annie's death at the Red Lion Inn on Monday 1st March, the jurymen gave up their fee to the Widow Leeson, and a public collection reaching around £12 was gathered for her. She never recovered her health – the tragedy was too much.

Meanwhile, William Stevens was still at his home, a wall thickness away from his victim's family, slowly but surely recovering from his self-inflicted wounds. He was, of course, under police guard and had managed to whisper a full confession to Superintendent Giles, head of the borough police. What wasn't known was why William felt he had to go so far to appease his anger over his unrequited love for Annie Leeson.

He was full of remorse and said to his police guard, 'I wish Mr De'ath had been out and I should have been dead and should have been in Heaven with my dear Annie.' But then he told another policeman, 'I spoke to her as civil as a man could speak, but she would not speak to me, and swung about, and then I done it.' This mixture of self-pity and anger at Annie's rejection continued to be expressed as the days went by but still he was too weak to be committed to gaol. Almost two weeks elapsed after the murder and Stevens was still 'in a prostrate state' at home. The local papers began pushing hard for his transfer to gaol and a trial for murder. He had not yet been before magistrates to be charged or enter a plea, but the media was not letting this stop them.

The *Bucks Advertiser and Aylesbury News* for 12th March 1864 said:

'The wretched young man Stevens who murdered the girl Leeson is still alive and improving in health. The wounds which he inflicted upon his throat have been so carefully attended to by Dr De'ath as to now enable the criminal to swallow solid food. There is now therefore every probability of his soon being able to be removed from the house of his parents to the Borough Gaol.'

However, it was not until Monday 18th July at Aylesbury's Lent assizes that Stevens was deemed fit enough to stand trial.

William John Stevens, 25, tailor, was charged with the wilful murder of Annie Leeson at Buckingham on 27th February 1864. He was also charged on the coroner's inquisition with the same offence. To both indictments (whether by his choice or that of his defence lawyer hoping for a manslaughter verdict) Stevens answered in a firm voice, 'Not guilty.'

He was a slight figure dwarfed by the imposing court surroundings, a young man of fair complexion and what the reporters described as 'a rather mild expression of countenance, appearing very far from being a man likely to commit such a crime'. But it would have had to take a strange twist of fate for any judge or jury to find him other than guilty. Unrequited love cannot be a mitigating circumstance, however powerful and dangerous the emotion it creates. Was he insane?

Again, love and insanity do merge from time to time, but, legally, Stevens was quite sane. Indeed, for the prosecution it was clearly premeditated, maybe not intended at the time it occurred, but it was a plan in his head.

His defence lawyer, Mr Payne, blamed 'the demon jealousy', which he said had '… actuated him when he struck the fatal blow'. He gave a moving address to the jury, urging mercy.

After the judge's summing up, the jury required only 15 minutes to return the verdict of 'Guilty'. Donning the black cap, the judge pronounced the sentence of death and Stevens was led from the dock.

On Friday 5th August, as early as 5 am, people started to arrive outside the county gaol in Bierton Road, Aylesbury. A continuous stream of people flooded into the area, estimated at around 3,000 by 8 am. Many young women were present as well as babes in arms and toddlers. The fearful sight of executioner Calcraft appeared, his trademark long flowing beard adding to the grim ceremony of death about to take place. Parents pointed him out to young children, 'Behave or Calcraft will get you' was a favourite threat to an unruly child. Calcraft was truly the stuff of nightmares and William John Stevens' final nightmare was about to begin.

'Help me O Lord, Lord help me now,' cried Stevens, and then it was all over.

The crowd started to drift away, about 100 or so waiting for the body to be cut down in an hour's time. Baskets of provisions were opened and many spectators enjoyed their picnic breakfasts. Vendors of ballads and 'dying speeches' of other prisoners moved among the crowds looking for customers.

Stevens was left hanging to await his second fate of being buried in unconsecrated prison ground and covered with hot lime to eat his body away as fast as possible to ensure he would not enter Heaven to be reunited with his dear Annie.

There is another distasteful part to this public death ceremony that was reported by Superintendent Symington. Immediately after Stevens was cut down, a man from Winslow asked if he could be allowed to rub his son's face and neck with the dead man's hand. His son had a scrofulous condition and the doctors had given up any hope of curing him so this was his last chance to try what is rumoured to be an ancient cure – the touch of evil – the affliction of his son being transferred to the murderer. He said he was able to pay any sum of money necessary. Superintendent Symington would not tolerate this distasteful, superstitious practice and was determined that the county should not be associated with such a barbaric ritual. He told the man in no uncertain terms to go home and not to reveal to anyone that, as a Buckinghamshire man, he had made such a request.

William Stevens' vicious murder of young Annie Leeson could only have ended in his death by judicial hanging. That day in

August 1864, however, not only marked a murderer's punishment for his terrible, tragic crime, which blighted the life of the community and the families involved, but also gave him the dubious distinction of being the very last prisoner to undergo a public execution in the county of Buckinghamshire.

LIKE A RAT IN A TRAP

───────── ❀ ─────────

Crimes of past centuries always hold a fascination for the contemporary reader for at least two interesting reasons. One is how little human nature has changed. Greed, lust and sheer wickedness are, unfortunately, always with us. Most modern crimes have been mirrored in past times, certainly as far as motive is concerned. It seems, however, that we learn little from them, and victims today are as vulnerable and exploited as they ever were in the past. In a strange way we can find that satisfying. We are very much as human as we've always been. The other reason for our fascination is precisely to see the changes that have occurred. For example, the public spectacle of a hanging as both entertainment and a deterrence, possibly followed by the display of the prisoner's body on a gibbet until it is putrid and finally just a skeleton, no longer features in our lives.

There well may be cries to bring back the death penalty for certain acts of murder, but we know that public hangings, ritualistic exhibitions and displaying bodies on gibbets are consigned to history.

The case of Edward Corbet and the Bierton murder of 1773 is a landmark one in that it was the last time the gibbet was used in Buckinghamshire. For that reason alone it is worth one more visit, particularly as the executed Mr Corbet, or rather parts of him, literally hung around the village into the next century, his skull outlasting the disintegrating irons that had caged him. Generations of villagers would pass him every day, even incorporating him into any travel directions they would give to passing strangers. 'You want the Hulcott road you say? Pass the Chalk-house Arms, turn to your left by the horse trough, keep ahead until you see Corbet's Piece then turn right and you'll be on the Hulcott road.'

In terms of his crime, nothing has changed. Killing someone to steal their possessions takes us nowhere new. However, in Corbet's case there was an ingredient that will always be appreciated whatever the century. This ingredient is variously called poetic justice or just desserts and Corbet certainly got his in a very unexpected way.

Corbet lived in Tring, just across the Buckinghamshire/ Hertfordshire border, and he worked as a rat-catcher and a chimney sweep. Both services were always in demand and farmers in particular would get him to clear the rats out of their barns. In early June 1773 Mr Richard Holt, a farmer in Bierton, Buckinghamshire employed Corbet to catch the rats on his farm.

Corbet's success as a rat-catcher was due in large part to his hard working dog who, on his master's command, would shoot like a rocket into the bundles of hay, chasing out the rats which Corbet would catch in a large sack, picking them up with his bare hands as fast as he could. Many more would be killed by his dog in the chase. A good dog with rats was worth a great deal in earning potential.

Sometimes Corbet would take ferrets up with him, usually borrowed on the promise of some payment once the farmer had paid him. He would occasionally accept payment in kind rather than cash, for example, salted pork, chicken and beef. If he was lucky, he would be paid two pence a rat and in a farmyard you could make upwards of four shillings on a good day.

Some rat-catchers would even pit themselves against a dog, getting down on their hands and knees and killing them with their teeth as a dog would. Whether Corbet did this or not is not recorded but a well-known rat-catcher (he preferred 'rat-killer') from Iver in Bucks is recorded as saying, 'I'm the man as they say kills rats – that's to say, I kills 'em like a dog, with my teeth.'

Corbet's small white bull-terrier dog was precious to him and he treated it quite well; it was after all earning him money. It wasn't much bigger than some of the rats it encountered and that was always a danger for the rat-catcher. A dog could be seriously infected through a rat bite, canker in the mouth being a common result, so Corbet would use peppermint and water to rinse out his dog's mouth when it was working.

'Dead 'un! Drop it!' he'd shout as soon as his dog had 'nosed' a rat.

When he was working at this particular farm, Mr Holt's, he began to think of other ways he could make money besides working for it. On June 4th the farmer's unmarried daughter,

Mary, who had been very ill, suddenly died and Mr Holt, a widower, was grieving very badly at the tragic loss of his only child. He was not in a position to check up on Corbet's work, just wishing to be left alone to grieve. He was at a very vulnerable time in his life and the rat-catcher planned to take advantage of this.

On a dark night Corbet crept to the farmhouse and, peering through the candle-lit window, saw Richard Holt praying before the coffin containing his recently deceased daughter. It was 7th June, three days before her funeral was due to take place. Corbet waited patiently until the distraught farmer took to his bed and then fetching his ladder used his skills as a chimney sweep to climb down the large open chimney into the farmer's bedroom. He crept about the room, intending to steal whatever valuables he could lay his hands on.

Mr Holt was asleep and, like the rats he was so familiar with, Corbet could have quietly scuttled past unseen, but he wanted to leave nothing to chance and bludgeoned the farmer to death. It was a cold-blooded, premeditated murder.

After scouring the farmhouse for valuables and collecting his spoils in his rat sack, he scampered out of the front door, closing it behind him so no one would suspect a break in, stored the ladder away, and set off home for Tring across the county border.

Early the next morning, the milk boy arrived at the house. He knew of the tragedy of Mary's death and thought that Mr Holt must be in great sorrow or distress not to answer the door. Worried that he couldn't get a response, he went to the nearby cottage where they had a key.

When the door was opened, a small white bull-terrier trotted out. If a dog could be puzzled this one probably was. He'd shot straight in the house as soon as his master had opened the door the night before, cleared the rats as he should but found he was trapped inside the house. At last his master had come for him. The neighbours, discovering a blood trail to Richard Holt's brutally beaten body in the same house as Corbet's dog, felt it was too much of a coincidence.

Encouraging the dog to 'find your master', the hastily summoned village constable together with an assortment of locals followed it all the way home to Tring. Corbet was arrested with some of Mr Holt's stolen property on him. His little dog, no doubt, ran delightedly around, pleased that he had not only

The bedroom where, on 7th June 1773, Richard Holt met his death

caught the rats his master set him to clear, but had also brought some friends along to see him.

Corbet's guilt was a foregone conclusion; the key witness may have only been able to bark but it was as good as a speech by the prosecution. The rat-catcher was found guilty and condemned to the gallows and then to be hung on a gibbet. The Bierton gibbet that was erected was large enough to serve as a gallows to execute the prisoner and then as a gibbet from which a cage containing his body could be suspended for all to see and take heed.

The spectacle of an 18th century hanging was an excuse for all kinds of merry making, laughter and excitement. Village executions were pure theatre and small market stalls would be set up selling refreshments and snacks such as nuts or meat puddings known as 'trotters', possibly some sparrow pie, and for the kids, candies, lemonade and maybe even some refreshing peppermint water, the very stuff Corbet used to keep his dog's mouth free from the effects of rat bites. Now the dog had ratted on him and on this 23rd day of July 1773 Corbet arrived, tied and bound in the hangman's cart to the cheers and boos of the waiting Bierton crowd.

The 18 ft gibbet ensured that no one's view was blocked as the cart was pulled from under him to rapturous applause. When death was officially pronounced by the local doctor, the body was encased in a tight-fitting iron cage and hung high up on the gibbet's arm where it could be seen for miles around. The worst part of this highly symbolic deterrent was yet to come. After the celebrations of the day, the body began to rot and putrefy over the following weeks and there was no mistaking the horrific stench for those downwind from the gibbet.

The hanging was in the last shout of July and this promised to be a long hot summer in Bierton.

Cottage windows had to stay shut, and the first sight many children saw on a sunny morning sitting up in bed would be Corbet rotting on the gibbet. Poor Mary Lane who lived as a servant in the farmhouse adjoining Mr Holt's farm, where the terrible murder took place, had no other view from her room unless she blocked up her window altogether.

The smell transcended the village and even reached high up into the farm cottages overlooking Bierton. It was reported that some villagers were unable to open their windows until after the harvest the following year. One cannot imagine, therefore, why, still in 1773, a local shepherd was said to have accepted half-a-crown from a betting stranger staying at the inn to climb up to Corbet, and put black gloves on his hands and a scarf around his face. The mission was accomplished but that old shepherd certainly earned his money for such a disgusting feat.

It seems that the deterrent value soon gives way to a village health hazard and this would be the last time such villagers in Buckinghamshire would be tortured in this way. Corbet was a wicked man, yet after death was still able to create victims out of a whole community by his disgusting smell and the sight of his maggot-ridden body.

Villagers even created a new footpath that ran from the Chalk-house Arms along the back of the poorer cottages to avoid having to walk past the corner of the field now known as Corbet's Piece. It is recorded that carriages would try and use this narrower, more unsuitable route in preference to passing the remains of the hanging rat-catcher next to the newly named Gib Lane.

Gib Lane, Bierton, is the only reminder that the 18ft high gibbet was sited near here

But the law had to take its due course, and he hung there for well over 22 years, all told. By that time, just his skull was left inside the rotting irons and that stayed put for many years after until it fell through the dilapidated metal bars and was kicked into the ditch as a final insult.

The gibbet remained, therefore, as a symbol of Corbet's wicked deed, for a long time into the Victorian age. It was partly disintegrating from natural decay but also from the depredations of certain brave villagers following old folk lore which claimed that if you removed a small piece of wood from a gibbet and rubbed it on your gums it would cure toothache. Its eventual fate in 1860 was to be taken down altogether and turned into Bierton gibbet souvenirs – pieces of the very last gibbet to be used in Buckinghamshire.

It was not, however, to be symbolic of the last wicked and callous murder that the county would see. Some things change; others, unfortunately, do not.

THE DISAPPEARING
RAMBLER

---❁---

One warm spring afternoon in the new millennium, I was busy setting up runner bean canes in our small kitchen garden at the back of our Prestwood home. Jan, my wife, was engrossed in sorting out the soft fruit bed in readiness for netting against marauding magpies.

It was pleasant and peaceful. Our views across a neighbouring field to a woodland backdrop was one to savour and enjoy.

It was Jan who heard him first.

'Excuse me, excuse me.'

She looked up, as did I on the second 'excuse me', and there, leaning over the small three-bar fence from the neighbouring field, was a stranger. We were both slightly taken aback as there is no right of way in the field and the only visitor we are used to seeing leaning over the fence is Tom, a neighbour's horse.

'Excuse me,' he continued, 'I am looking for Church Path. I am very sorry to trouble you but I appear to be lost.'

He was quite a short man, dressed in a very unusual style. He was wearing a complete tweed suit with old-fashioned knickerbocker style trousers tucked into diamond-patterned socks and, on his feet, large, bulbous leather walking boots. He had a map case hanging around his neck like a big label and, most incongruous of all, was a small hat with a feather in the rim. It reminded us both of what we could only call an Alpine or Swiss style hat that you sometimes see in old films or storybooks. He had a touch of P.G. Wodehouse's Bertie Wooster about him.

Jan politely told him that indeed he was lost as this was private land and to reach Church Path he would need to return across the field and climb back into the woodland. If he then kept walking to his right, following the path that meandered between the trees, he would come to Church Path. I was dying to ask him why he was dressed in that fashion, but thought better of it and said nothing.

One thing that I do recall, that I didn't quite place at the time, was that you couldn't catch his eye. He did not actually look at us, he seemed rather to be asking his question in our general direction.

'Thank you, thank you, sorry to have troubled you.'

He touched his feathered hat, turned on his heel and walked briskly across the field. We stood and watched him reach the woodland, and, climbing onto the fence, he disappeared into the wood. Jan and I looked at each other. She laughed and said what a strange little man he was and added, 'Did you notice how he didn't look at us when he spoke?'

'How did he get to us?' I wondered. 'You can't get lost looking for Church Path and finish up outside our garden. Church Path is clearly marked on all the local walking maps.'

We agreed it was strange but he wasn't someone you would regard as suspicious, just odd. We continued to enjoy a very pleasant afternoon's gardening.

The next day was just as fine and my son Paul was working with me, sawing up some logs for our wood store, which was very low after a cold winter. Over the sound of sawing, I heard a familiar voice: 'Excuse me, excuse me.'

I looked up and there he was, tweed knickerbockers, map case, Swiss hat, standing exactly where he had stood the afternoon before. Paul saw me looking, stopped and turned around just in time to hear the stranger say, 'Excuse me, I am looking for Church Path. I am very sorry to trouble you but I appear to be lost.'

I couldn't believe what I was seeing and hearing. Had I gone mad? Was yesterday's encounter merely a dream? This was serious deja vu.

Paul didn't hesitate to walk across to the fence and explain to this strange little man that he had to go back across the field, over the fence into the wood and keep to the right. It was as if time was momentarily frozen whilst I fathomed out what to do or say. Was this a practical joke?

Instead of challenging him, I let Paul redirect him, hearing the now familiar 'Thank you, thank you, sorry to have troubled you.' We watched him head for the woodland fence. I tried to explain to Paul that exactly the same thing had happened yesterday, at the same spot and about the same time. Understandably, he couldn't quite grasp what I was going on about and gave me an old-fashioned look when I suggested that we follow our visitor.

The stranger had just reached the fence to climb over into the woods when we set off across the field at top speed. By the time we reached the fence, only a matter of seconds had passed. At that point in the woods you can clearly see another 150 yards or so ahead, so he was bound to be in view. Paul was ahead of me and disappeared over the fence just moments after the stranger. I followed and found him standing still, clearly puzzled.

'He's gone,' he said, 'disappeared.'

'He can't have,' I replied, 'no one could have got out of sight for another couple of minutes.'

We looked around but could see neither hide nor hair of him. But, when we were climbing back over the fence into the field, there was something that looked familiar. It was a small white, fluffy feather, just like the one I had noticed in his hat. It was resting on the bottom bar of the fence. I picked it up – it seemed that I should.

Paul was ahead of me, I said nothing about the feather and put it into my jacket pocket.

The stranger never did reappear and ask for Church Path again, at least not when any of us were in the garden. I kept thinking about how he had seemed to be addressing his question to others that he could see in our garden, but that would be silly, wouldn't it?

Then, about six months later, over a beer, I mentioned the story to a retired farmer friend. He was totally matter-of-fact about it. 'Oh, that'll be Stan, the map man. Swiss Stan as some folks call him on account of his hat.'

I waited for the joke, for the wind-up, but it didn't come.

Apparently, about the turn of the 19th century, according to my farmer, inspired by the pioneering work of the Commons, Open Spaces and Footpaths Preservation Society (now the Open Spaces Society), Stanley developed an obsession with mapping the common land and foothpaths of Buckinghamshire. He would be seen by village and farm folk wandering great distances all over the district making his maps. His outfit was very fashionable at the time and his hat as distinctive then as today.

'And he was going around making his maps in 1900? But the man we saw was in his fifties. How would you know about him anyway?' I asked. 'You're seventy-five, so you weren't born until 1925.'

The fence over which the rambler disappeared into the wood

He was a local legend, the old farmer told me. Both his dad and granddad would speak of him. Although farmers and ramblers were not the best of friends, Stan's maps were of use to all sorts of country folk in those days. He might have been a bit eccentric but he was well thought of.

I asked what happened to him.

It seems that a tragic accident killed him one spring afternoon while he was mapping a local footpath. He'd got lost and had fallen while climbing over a fence into woodland up at Prestwood. He had cracked his head badly, which caused internal bleeding. It was some days before he was found by a local gardener, who had only spoken to him a few days earlier when he had asked his way as he was lost.

I hardly dared think about it.

At home, I felt in the pocket of my old gardening jacket and my fingers touched the fluffy texture of a small white feather.

THE MURDER IN THE COW HOUSE

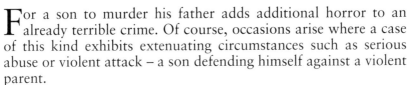

For a son to murder his father adds additional horror to an already terrible crime. Of course, occasions arise where a case of this kind exhibits extenuating circumstances such as serious abuse or violent attack – a son defending himself against a violent parent.

The crime of parricide, as it is called, is a rare one, so when it occurs it tends to attract far more attention than most. The case of William Francis Adams of Burcott in Buckinghamshire was far from straightforward and to this day leaves a mystery behind.

Did 18 year old William Adams murder his father, Thomas, in cold blood at Fox Cover Hill cow house, Burcott on the afternoon of Thursday 28th December 1837? Were there issues between them that have never been revealed? Some say William was set up, a victim of a conspiracy by others to deflect their guilt at involvement in robbing and killing the wealthy local farmer.

The *Aylesbury Gazette* of 17th March 1838 aptly expressed the dilemma that occupied the inhabitants of the hamlet of Burcott and, indeed, the parish of Wing and beyond when it commented that:

'… the youth was either perfectly innocent and consequently much injured; or that he was the most depraved, hardened and reckless of men …'

Which was he? This unsolved Buckinghamshire murder would have been easily settled by the forensic science of modern times, but in 1838 it was down to witness statements and old-fashioned policing. So what was the evidence at the time and what will your verdict be on the murder in the cow house?

What happened on that December day will, of course, never be fully known, as the act of murder itself was not witnessed. It was the circumstantial evidence that would later be presented in court that was responsible for the eventual verdict.

Old Mr Adams, as he was called, was a wealthy and, some would say, eccentric farmer, who owned a great deal of land and property in the Burcott and Wing area of Buckinghamshire. He had eleven children: two sons and nine daughters. Some folk felt he was a harsh and sometimes violent man towards his children but evidence of this was sketchy at most. It was known, however, that his eldest son, William, did have some serious rows with his father. Old Mr Adams had frequently been heard to say that his son '… would no more mind shooting me than a dog'. There was, indeed, some evidence that William did have angry feelings towards his father. In the spring of the year his father was murdered, when William was only 17 years old, Hannah Jordan, one of the farm labourers' wives, saw William observe his father in the distance and heard him say, 'Yonder he is coming; damn him, I wish somebody would blow his bloody brains out.'

In past years, William had stormed out of the farm and stayed with friends until the current row with his father blew over. Once when he was only 16, he went to stay with William Judge, under game-keeper to Lord Chesterfield, for a few days. His father had accused William of loading his gun with clay so it would explode and kill him. However, things seemed to have settled down and in early December 1837 he told his friend William Judge that things were going okay and he hadn't fallen out with his father since 1st September.

So what exactly did happen on the afternoon of Thursday 28th December 1837?

Around 3 pm that day, George Bone, Old Mr Adams' horse-keeper, was carrying dung to a field called Broad Stitching when he saw his master on his black mare coming along the Soulbury road. It was a little unusual for at this time the mare was usually out to graze. The farmer cut a distinct figure, tall in the saddle and with his familiar broad-brimmed felt hat. He rode on towards Fox Cover Hill. George also saw William Adams some distance away, walking across the turnip field. He thought no more about it and carried on with his work. Nearby, in an area called Home Ground, Matthew Collier, John Hopcraft, David Bull, Thomas Jordan and Thomas Leys were also busy working for their master. William Adams had sauntered past them carrying a single-barrelled shotgun. Two loud reports filled the air as the five farm labourers saw him go into Turfmoor, shoot at some larks and a snipe and then set off along the brook towards the turnip field leading to Fox Cover Hill.

No sooner was William out of sight, than his father rode up on his black mare, greeted his workers, and rode off across the hill towards Briar Furlong Pasture, also en route to Fox Cover Hill. About 30 minutes after they had lost sight of William and his father, they all heard another shot let loose from the direction of the turnip field and then, about 10 minutes after that, a fourth shot split the air from the direction of the fish pond which lies just below Fox Cover Hill cow house.

Only minutes after the last report had faded, William Adams was seen by Matthew Collier and his fellow workers, riding his father's black mare at full trot along Home Ground in the direction of the farmhouse. It was unusual, but no doubt his dad had sent him on an errand back to the house.

Around 5 pm the workers packed up for the day and went home.

George Bone saw William arrive back at the farm on Old Mr Adams' mare just before dusk. He stayed in the stable talking to George for about 30 minutes. He explained how he'd arranged to meet up with his father at the cow house on Fox Cover Hill to treat some sheep with foot root. They'd completed this and his father said he'd rather walk back and asked William to ride the mare home. George knew that on rare occasions Old Mr Adams had been out at night, but usually he kept his horse with him and would not want to be on foot in the fields after dark. William also warned George that his father suspected him of stealing corn from the new barn and he was checking up on him. George asked permission to leave the farm for some personal business in Leighton that evening. William said he could go the next evening but should stay at the farm that night because he himself was off to a psalm-singing feast at Wing. 'My father will not like us both to be absent together,' he explained. He then added he wondered where his father had got to as he should be at home by now for his tea.

That evening, William was out on the town, laughing, drinking and dancing with young Rebecca Carter at the Cock pub in Wing. His friend William Judge joined him for a beer and rum drinking session. He told Judge that he'd been out shooting snipe that day and that his father had not come home by the time he'd

The Cock Inn at Wing, where William Adams was a regular customer

gone out. William decided to go back to see if his father had returned, so he left the pub and arrived back at the farm at around 8.30 pm.

George Bone said the master was still missing, so William sent George back to Wing to find William Judge to help in a search. George tracked Judge down to the Six Bells and they returned to the farm together. William told Judge that he had left his father at Broad Stitching gate as he had intended going to the new barn, which was only about 400 yards further on, to keep a watch on the horse-keeper. William then suggested they investigate the immediate farm buildings but leave any more distant search until the next day. He added that his sisters were crying and very upset that their father had not returned home. William, his younger brother Henry, Judge and Bone decided to call on Judge senior, Richard Judge, the game-keeper for Lord Chesterfield, for advice.

They set off for his house in Burcott. William told Mr Judge that his father had been missing since he left him at Broad Stitching that afternoon and he had been sent home with the mare. Richard Judge took his lantern and went with his son, the two Adams boys and George Bone to the new barn.

Old Mr Adams was certainly not there. William then mentioned that his father had said something about visiting one of his tenants, Mr Burgess at Rock Lane, so they called on Mr Burgess, who said he had not met up with William's father that day. They also called on Thomas Worster, one of the labourers, to ask if he had seen his master that evening but he hadn't. They then decided to check all the local pubs, again with no luck. After that their attention was directed around the rickyard and stables. Again no luck.

Richard Judge decided they ought to check out the cow house at Fox Hill Cover, as that was the last place William had been working with his father. William agreed.

When they arrived at the cow house, William immediately said that the hay had been moved since he had been there that afternoon. There was no door to the cow house, just a hurdle across the open entrance, and hay was spilling out over the threshold. Judge senior moved the hurdle aside, hung his lantern on a beam and started to pull away trusses of clover hay, then jumped back exclaiming: 'Oh my God, here he is poor soul – poor creature.'

William rushed forward crying, 'Oh my poor father, what shall I do?' He then stumbled as if to faint and Judge junior, Henry and George Bone had to support him.

The flickering lantern shed its orange glow across a gruesome sight. Thomas Adams lay on his back with his legs crossed, his clothes covered with hay that had stuck to the river of blood that had cascaded down from where his head used to be. It had been blasted away at close range by a shotgun. As the newspapers were later to report, '... his head had been literally blown to atoms'.

It was now about 11.30 pm; Bone took another lantern from the cow house and rushed off to organise a waggon and horses to collect the body of his master. William Adams was distraught and had to be comforted by his companions. About an hour later George had returned with William Denchfield, publican of the Six Bells at Wing. The landlord checked the dead farmer's pockets for the safe-keeping of any personal possessions, found nothing more than a tobacco box and then assisted in lifting the bloodied and stiff corpse into the waggon, and they all set off back to the farmhouse.

It was 2 am on a bitterly cold Friday morning, 29th December, that Mr Richard Olley, a surgeon from Leighton Buzzard, arrived at the farm. He instructed that the body of Thomas Adams should be taken inside the house for examination. With some difficulty, he prised the felt hat away from what remained of the dead farmer's skull. The blast of a shotgun at close range into the back of the neck, through the brim of the hat, had created a gruesome muddle of broken bones, congealed blood, spinal marrow, gun shot, and pieces of felt. They had been driven straight through the head, exiting through the poor man's nostrils. Small pieces of Mr Adams' mackintosh collar and felt hat were also found embedded in sections of his brain.

This would be the first of a series of thorough post-mortems that day, first by Richard Olley at the farm, then by Mr Ceely at Aylesbury and again by another surgeon, Mr Wagstaff, to collect all the facts for the coroner. The most important discovery was by Mr Wagstaff when he located the actual pellet that killed Mr Adams lodged in brain tissue. The conclusion of all the medical men was that Thomas Adams died from one gun shot fired at close range from behind.

Friday morning daylight at the cow house had revealed much more than the previous night's lantern light could. It appeared that

Old Mr Adams had fallen backwards outside the cow house, as there was blood about a foot and a half from the threshold, carefully concealed with clover hay. However, there were no marks of a body being dragged into the cow house itself. As the news of Old Mr Adams' murder travelled round the district, folk from miles around started to arrive at the cow house to see the crime scene for themselves.

Sergeant Samuel Perkins of Aylesbury police conducted the inquiry and had no shortage of witness statements. So many farm workers had seen father and son that Thursday afternoon heading in the same direction, William on foot with a gun, his father on his black mare. They confirmed the sound of gun shots and that William had returned alone riding his father's horse shortly afterwards. The sergeant was told of old arguments between father and son and of accusations and violent tempers on both sides.

At 5 pm on Friday evening Sergeant Perkins interviewed William Adams and his brother-in-law, Mr Hedges, at the farmhouse. William told the police officer that he could not help with any information. He had left his father in the cow house and was told to take his horse home. His father had said a walk would do him good and he would go to the barn to watch George Bone, who was stealing corn for his horses. William then mysteriously added, 'I have a witness.'

Sergeant Perkins replied, 'What do you mean, a witness?'

'To prove that I never fired the gun.'

To which Perkins said, 'Do you mean the gun that shot your father?'

'Yes,' said William.

'Has anybody accused you?' asked Perkins.

'No,' replied William, 'but I thought by your questions, you suspect me.'

Perkins then asked William to walk with him for a serious talk. They headed towards Wing, the sergeant speaking frankly about what he had discovered that day. He turned to William and said: 'You were the last person with your father, you came home with his horse, you were out with a gun, you had powder and shot and your father is found shot in the cow house. At what time, William, did you leave your father at the cow house?'

'About half-past three,' replied William.

They both headed back to the farm, William agreeing to further questioning the following morning.

Later that evening, Sergeant Perkins, mulling over all the facts in his possession, decided William was right: he was the prime suspect, and should be arrested as such. He went to the farm. William was not there. He took three farm workers to help find him, the first stop being the Six Bells. William was not there either. Then, looking along the road, Perkins spotted two figures heading towards Burcott. As Perkins approached them, they started running. The police officer caught up with them and seized one by the collar.

It was William Adams. He let the other go; it was, no doubt, his friend, William Judge.

William agreed to co-operate and went with the sergeant to the Cock pub at Wing. There the police officer searched him and found a crumpled checked handkerchief with dried bloodstains. It appeared to have recently been washed but not very successfully. He also found a gun-punch, percussion caps, one pellet, a snuff box, two knives, three shillings, and some pence. The inside of William's shooting jacket was very bloody. William said it was the blood of a hare he killed a fortnight ago. Perkins thought differently; it looked too fresh.

William Adams was arrested and kept under police guard at the Cock to await the coroner's investigation, due to start there the following day. On Saturday morning, whilst the coroner was organising his jury, William was asked by the police if he knew what money or valuables his father was likely to have had on him. William thought he could have been carrying as much as £60 in a mixture of sovereigns and notes. His father tended to carry large sums of cash in a brown purse tucked into his breeches.

Sergeant Perkins went back up to the cow house and conducted a thorough search, finding Old Mr Adams' watch hidden under some hay. It had been decided by the coroner to adjourn the inquest until Monday. Meanwhile Sergeant Perkins had made a further significant discovery. The pellet extracted from Thomas Adams' brain fitted the gun-punch he had taken from his son. It was not looking good for William Adams.

The coroner's hearing was detailed and long. It began on Monday and finished on Tuesday evening. As expected, the evidence from all witnesses placed William in the position of prime suspect but it was the evidence from labourer Thomas Worster that clinched it.

Before Sergeant Perkins had located and arrested him on Friday evening, it was learnt that William had gone to Worster's house around 7 pm and the following conversation had taken place.

'Worster,' said William, 'if I can't get you, or someone to swear that you saw my father and me part on Fox Cover Hill, I am a done man.'

Worster replied, 'God bless me, Master William, you don't say so.'

'I do though,' said William. 'I must go for the policemen are after me.'

This was, no doubt what William was banking on when he told Sergeant Perkins that he had a witness. He was gambling on Worster giving him an alibi.

Worster, however, was to make things far worse with his next revelation. He claimed that on the evening of the murder, before it was discovered, William had gone to him and said, 'Worster, you need not go to the cow house tonight to turn out the sheep, for I have done it myself.' Worster replied, 'Your father has ordered me, Master William, to do it every night.'

'Ah, well,' said William, 'you need not go tonight.'

A little later, William again went to Worster and said, 'I have been again and seen to the sheep so that you need not go.' Worster again pleaded that he had orders from his father. William becoming angry said firmly to end the matter, 'I tell you, you must not go.' Worster obeyed and did not go to the cow house at Fox Cover Hill that night.

With such witness evidence and the fact that the pellet found in the victim's brain exactly fitted the gun-punch used by William, the coroner's jury returned a verdict of wilful murder. On Wednesday 3rd January 1838 Adams was committed for trial at the forthcoming assizes and sent to Aylesbury Gaol.

The parish was divided. How could a son kill his father like that? He must be the most wicked and depraved individual. Others who knew William reminded folk that he was innocent until proven guilty and he was never a violent lad. What was his motive? He would inherit the farm anyway. The gossip was continuous and the newspapers teetered on the edge of libellous statements to get a good story – and this was good story.

Under the headline 'The Alleged Parricide', the *Aylesbury News* in its lead story of 13th January 1838, said: 'From information obtained from persons residing in the neighbourhood of Wing who were well acquainted with the deceased and his family, it appears that he was of a very violent temper, and that he was continually quarrelling, not only with the prisoner, but also with all his other children of whom there are ten, nine girls and a boy. It is said that the prisoner has, at various times, exhibited symptoms of insanity, but has never been under any restraint.'

A violent father killed by his insane son would certainly be a story they would love to print. It seemed an age to the March assizes and the local tension was palpable. The Burcott murder, as it was now known, was expected to draw record crowds at the Aylesbury assizes when the case was heard on Friday 9th March. Six hundred special tickets were issued for admittance to the court but the rush through the doors was so great that fighting broke out between those desperate to get in and the court's javelin-men, armed with pikes. Some injuries occurred as a result.

Eighteen year old William Adams, upon being arraigned, spoke clearly and loudly: 'Not guilty,' he said.

The prosecution was extremely well organised. It did, after all, have all those farm workers' witness statements putting William in the right location with a gun and the sound of gun shots. There was also the gun punch that matched the pellet that killed his father, and his alleged conversations with Worster. And why had he run away from Sergeant Perkins if he wasn't guilty?

Then a surprise witness for the prosecution was called, one James Fuel.

Fuel was a prisoner in Aylesbury Gaol with Adams and claimed that William had confessed the murder of his father to him. Gasps of surprise filled the court, and the noise of conversations from the public gallery brought the javelin-men back into action. Fuel claimed that William told him that his father had accused him of stealing £10 and had said he would send him to gaol. William then planned the cow house visit on the Thursday in Christmas week with his father to treat some sheep for foot rot. After the work was done and just as his father was leaving the cow house to pull turnips for the sheep, William shot him in the back part of the neck.

Fuel then claimed William told him that he had taken his father to the further side of the cow house, and laid him on his back.

The pocket book was hidden in this privy, which is still standing on the farm at Burcott

Seeing his father's arm move, he loaded the gun once more and shot him in the face. He rifled his pockets, taking money contained in a pocket book, and a purse, covered his father with hay, and rode his horse home. He hid the pocket book in a nearby hedge on the way. Next morning, he retrieved the pocket book with the money and hid it over the privy and covered it with a tile. He also had eleven sovereigns and a half and the key to his father's desk, which he had found in the purse, so he hid this in the roots of dahlia plant outside the farmhouse.

Under cross-examination, a different context for Fuel's statement was teased out by William's defence lawyer, Mr Kelly. 30 year old Fuel claimed: 'I said to Mr Sheriff that if it could do me any good, it was not my duty to cloak it; it would ease my mind and lighten my own case; a good many folk get clear by giving evidence against others.'

Mr Kelly began his defence against what appeared to be an inevitable guilty verdict. So far, the jury had been inundated with damning evidence against William. Kelly, however, was a man of precision and knew exactly where the flaw in the prosecution's evidence lay. It had been totally missed up to that point. It was the timing of the final gun shot and the precise location of his client when it was heard.

Firstly, he was able to dismiss the gun-punch match made so much of by the police. When he cross-examined Richard Judge, the game-keeper admitted that his gun-punch was exactly the same size as the prisoner's and he had often cut wadding for William as well as his father, as well as loaning his own gun-punch. 'Many gun-punches are the same size,' he explained.

Then for the next three hours, Mr Kelly pursued his key point. The last two shots heard coming from the direction of the cow house were said by a succession of defence witnesses to have occurred after 5 pm, not before. The first two shots were of no consequence as they were clearly William shooting larks and snipe and his father was seen at that time anyway. It was the timing of the last two shots on which the whole murder charge rested. Kelly set out to prove that William had gone by the time the final shots were heard.

Farmer William Cook, labourer William Thorn, railway worker Henry Hounslow and other highly respected and reliable witnesses all put the timing of the significant final shot at around 5.15 pm on that day.

Another succession of witnesses said they saw William Adams around 4 pm that day in the vicinity of Wing. Elizabeth Newens saw William walking with William Judge at five minutes past four. Judge junior said he had met up with William going to Wing at around 4 pm. They both went to the Queen's Head and had two pints of ale, then to the Cock and had a glass of rum each. William's alibi grew stronger and stronger when Mary Windmill testified: 'My husband keeps the Queen's Head at Wing. On Thursday 28th December, the prisoner come to our house. It was a little after 4 pm. He left about half-past four; he returned at 6 pm and stayed until 8 pm.' Although this still left a time gap for William to slip back to the cow shed, this was mostly filled by the eminent William Mortimer, registrar at Wing, who confirmed seeing William singing in the Cock at twenty past four. He was still there when Mr Mortimer left.

All that remained to be done was to discredit the prisoner James Fuel, which was left to another group of witnesses who proclaimed him a congenital liar, and then others were brought forward to give character witnesses on behalf of William Adams.

The trial which had commenced at 9 am on Friday morning was now concluded at 4 am on Saturday morning. Nineteen continuous hours and the atmosphere was electric whilst the jury considered their verdict. After 20 minutes they returned. 'Not guilty,' said the foreman.

The court erupted. William was a free man ... but not for long. His ordeal was far from ended. The police had other ideas about his guilt. William Adams was rearrested and indicted with stealing a pocket book on 28th December 1837, the property of his deceased father, at the parish of Burcott.

James Fuel was to get his day in court once more in an attempt to secure his own freedom by giving further evidence against Adams.

The police were convinced that William had knowledge of how his father met his death, so, if he didn't do it, he knew who did. Stealing was a trivial offence compared to a parricide charge but the police hoped it would throw some light on what really happened on the afternoon of 28th December.

So on 26th July 1838, William Francis Adams found himself in the dock once more at Aylesbury assizes. The questions were many. Whilst in prison, did William Adams give James Fuel details of this crime, including a confession to stealing the pocket book and purse from his father? Did Fuel know of this crime and who was responsible for it before he met up with William in Aylesbury Gaol? Was William set up by Fuel's companions on the outside in order to find a scapegoat for the murder and robbery of old man Adams? Was Fuel just a liar hoping to get his own sentence quashed in exchange for evidence? The murder charge had failed, so what about the charge of stealing, which would put William at the scene of the murder once more? For once, the law was on his side as it stated that, having been found innocent of murdering his father, whatever was now said in court, he was safe from that charge ever being brought against him again. A person cannot be charged twice for the same offence after a verdict has been reached in the original trial.

Fuel said that William told him that when Mr Adams lay back dead, he took from his father a pocket book containing eight £5 notes, lots of bills and a purse with eleven sovereigns and a half and the key to his father's desk. Fuel claimed it was between 3 pm and 4 pm on Thursday 28th December and he repeated his story told at the murder trial about William hiding the pocket book first in the hedge and then the privy and the purse under the dahlia roots.

It was the next part to Fuel's story that took the silent court into new territory. He claimed William had asked him to help recover the money. Fuel said his brother Richard could take out some written instructions to others to secure the money for him. According to James Fuel, William wrote two notes, one large, one smaller, which he handed to James's brother Richard on visiting day.

As neither of the Fuels could read or write, they did not know exactly what the notes said, only what William told them he had written. Richard took the notes to his uncle, Robert Brown, a tailor at Denham, to read for him. He also showed them to Mary Ann Fuel, James's wife, and finally to Jane Shackle, the wife of friend John Shackle, at his house in Pinner. Then, it was claimed, the notes were burnt.

In court, Robert Brown, Mary Fuel and Jane Shackle agreed as to the contents and, from memory, all three recited the same version

The first, larger note Adams was alleged to have written said:

'This is to inform you where to get the money. Go to Wing, at Burcott, and inquire for Adams's farm. Go in the day time and look round and see where the privy is. On the right hand side, over the door, in a hole betwixt the tilings and the lock, you'll find a pocket book. Take the money out of the pocket book, and let the papers remain in, put in the little note and drop it down on the roadside against the Cock Inn, Wing.'

The second, smaller note Adams was alleged to have written, which was to be planted inside the pocket book before it was discarded outside the inn, said:

'The man you have got hold of is innocent. Them that done the deed you may find it out.'

The intended result, it was implied, was that someone finding the pocket book containing Farmer Adams' papers but no money would hand it in to the authorities. The police might then be swayed by the planted note to believe that the real thief, who could also be the real murderer, had a conscience and had left the note in order to clear William's name.

William's defence claimed that the notes were not written by William Adams at all but by an inmate called Meads in an attempt to frame William in a plot with Fuel for a crime he did not commit. Conveniently, Meads, who it was claimed knew where the money was hidden, had been transported so was not available to give evidence. Another inmate, Palmer, said it was done by Meads '... to spring a plant and clap it on Adams' back'.

Then the story entered new realms once again when landlord of the Red Lion at Tring, William Price, gave evidence that John Shackle, Richard Fuel and another had stayed at his pub the previous February, getting drunk and talking of their plot to retrieve a valuable hoard from the privy at the Adams' Farm at Burcott. The next morning, 28th February, Price went with a colleague, Thomas Jackson, to the farm and told Richard Fountain, brother-in-law of the prisoner, what he had heard.

Richard Fountain immediately went to the privy, looked into the hole over the roof and found the pocket book. He kept this find to himself until he handed it over to the magistrates only at the end of March, when the new charge of stealing had been laid against William.

Meanwhile later that day as the landlord, his colleague and now Adams' attorney, Mr Willis, discussed the matter and took tea in the farmhouse, the three men at the pub passed by their window in search of their bounty, which was now safely secreted in Fountain's pocket. He claimed it only contained three £5 country notes and one Bank of England £5 note.

After this twist in the tale, a whole succession of witnesses was called by the defence to proclaim James Fuel a liar, just trying to save his own neck.

The jury only took ten minutes to deliver their verdict against William Adams. It was 'Guilty'.

Audible gasps were heard all around the court. The judge turned to William, bidding him to use the remainder of his days to repent his dreadful crime and what he called his obdurate hardness of heart in rifling the bleeding body of his dead father and heartlessly appropriating the money of that parent for his own avarice with same ruthless cupidity as the murderer of his deceased parent could ever have expected to do. He regretted that the law only allowed him to pass a sentence of seven years transportation.

Was William that ruthless murderer after all or was convicted felon James Fuel's plan to frame him a partial success? No one was ever subsequently charged for the murder of Mr Thomas Adams at the hamlet of Burcott in the parish of Wing, Buckinghamshire.

What is your verdict?

MYSTERY, MOTIVE
AND MURDER AT
HANSLOPE PARK

---------❖---------

Some murders leave behind long-standing debates and mysteries about the true motive of the killer. The murder of Squire Edward Hanslope Watts on 21st July 1912 is such a case. In fact, it was conceivable the killer intended to claim two victims on that day, Squire Watts and his wife of 44 years, Edith Watts.

The weather was glorious, it was Sunday morning and the squire and his wife took their customary picturesque one and a half mile walk to the Sunday service at Hanslope parish church. Life was comfortable for them, residing in the stately home of Hanslope Park with its magnificent gardens and a large staff to care for them. He was the respected squire, magistrate and Lord of the Manor of Hanslope and Castlethorpe. Edith was a caring mother to their only daughter Irene, who had only left home recently to marry after living with them for 30 years. Now she busied herself running the large household of Hanslope Park with a delicate efficiency.

With the church bells inviting the local congregation to prayer, the squire and his wife entered the church; she sat towards the north side to take a more active part in singing hymns, whilst the squire took his usual place in the gallery pew where he could see and be seen. He was literally sitting on the family seat, below which was a vault containing the remains of his ancestors. He expected to join them one day, but at 67 felt he was good for quite a few years yet.

Greeting the vicar, villagers, and friends after the service, they set off again for the slow walk back, with the promise of roast beef and Yorkshire pudding washed down with a draught of best ale to help them on their way on this hot summer's day.

As was their usual custom, Squire Watts walked ahead of Edith, yet they conversed as if side by side. It was an odd arrangement but they were happy with it. As they strolled back to Hanslope Park, they met Dr Rutherford coming towards them on his bicycle. He was their family doctor as well as a friend, and after a pleasant chat, the doctor resumed his ride to the village, and once more the squire took the lead in the walk back to Hanslope Park.

Only a matter of minutes later, and just as they approached the lodge gates, the hazy summer peace was shattered by a gun shot from the left side of the road and the squire fell instantly forward to the ground. In that split second of the gun's deafening report, Edith saw a man crouching behind the hedge, a gun at his shoulder. With a scream of anguish and bewilderment, she rushed forward, flinging herself down at her husband's side to protect him. As she did so, a second shot rang out, hitting Squire Watts in his spine.

First on the scene was Mrs Green, the coachman's wife, who, on hearing the shots, looked through the lodge window and saw the squire in the road. Edith shouted for her to fetch help. Husband George Green was there in minutes, just as a third shot echoed through the summer air. Quickly George took in the situation. He ascertained that the squire was dead and headed off towards the trampled grass of the spinney, where the last shot seemed to come from. There he discovered the body of William Farrow, head game-keeper to Squire Watts, his head blown to pieces, a double-barrelled shotgun by his side.

Other locals, alerted by shouting and cries of murder, arrived on the scene, some rushing off to fetch the police. PC Cooper from Hanslope hurried along on his bike, closely followed by Dr Rutherford, who had passed that way only minutes earlier. Others arrived alerted by neighbours, including Robert Garratt from the St John's Ambulance Brigade. Mr Garratt immediately began caring for Mrs Watts who was uninjured but in great distress. Dr Rutherford certified that both the squire and the game-keeper were dead and then also tried to help the anguished Edith Watts. That summer Sunday had been shattered in minutes and so had Edith's life. The inquest at the Greyhound Inn, Tathall End was held the following day.

Mrs Farrow, the game-keeper's wife, recalled that her husband had left home at around 10 or 10.30 am, saying he was taking cartridges to one of Squire Watts' tenants. He had no gun with him. At Hanslope, game-keepers were forbidden to carry guns on a Sunday. Reluctantly, Mrs Farrow also admitted that her husband was very drunk. He had not been eating properly for days and had consumed vast quantities of primrose wine.

William Farrow had scribbled something in the game book, grabbed the cartridges and stumbled out of the door. Farrow's first port of call was at Manor Farm, where he met Mrs Mary Beesley. In her evidence, Mrs Beesley remembered Farrow saying: 'Will you give me a glass of beer to quench my thirst for I am parched.' She had poured him a half pint of ale. She recalled his glassy eyes and unnatural manner. She had become frightened when he began fiddling with her husband's gun lying inside the farmhouse doorway and then he demanded her husband's razor before 'they' came out of church. She told Farrow it was not right and he went.

Another game-keeper, Henry Martin, said Farrow had complained the previous December that lies were being spread about him. Dr Rutherford gave evidence that Farrow had suffered severe sun-stroke the summer before and that might induce a sudden apoplectic seizure. It also came to the jury's attention that Farrow had been under two weeks' notice from Squire Watts to quit for 'gross dereliction of duty'. So was this a revenge killing? The jury returned a verdict of wilful murder against Farrow and 'felo de se' (suicide) in relation to his own death. However, some mysteries remain to this day about Farrow's motive and state of mind. He had not told his wife he was under notice to quit and he had taken to drinking heavily as a result of his secret.

What did Squire Watts mean by 'gross dereliction of duty'?

Not long before that fateful day, the squire and his wife had gone abroad on holiday and Edith Watts had entrusted Farrow with the care of her much-loved retriever dog at his cottage. When they returned, the dog had died through neglect by Farrow. Mrs Watts was distraught and called him a murderer; Squire Watts gave him notice to quit.

In view of this episode, was Farrow's second shot intended for Edith Watts? When she threw herself forward to her husband's side as he fired the second shot did he think he had successfully hit her? He was found with one live cartridge still in the gun's breech and four in his pocket. So he had time and ammunition to fire again before he took his own life.

It was certainly a premeditated murder and not a spontaneous drunken episode as he had hidden his own gun in the spinney all week, borrowing another from James Ruff of Wood Farm. Why did he ask Mrs Beesley for a razor? He was hardly likely to want to shave before killing his victim or victims. Was this intended to be a weapon also?

On Friday 28th July 1912 Squire Watts was cremated and his ashes placed in the parish church under the family pew, where he had sat only the previous Sunday. Farrow was buried in a dark corner of the churchyard to be forgotten. Farrow's widow and three children had elicited sympathy from many people. It was not her doing and people did make a collection and lend a hand when necessary. However, such sympathy soon evaporated when Widow Farrow had a headstone placed on her husband's grave. On it was written:

'Waiting till all shall be revealed'

Locals saw no mystery here, it was an insult. Farrow was a murderer, there was nothing more to reveal. Police were obliged to guard the headstone against attack until emotions subsided.

Is there more to learn? What did Farrow write in the game book before he set off on his murderous mission. Just one word in a shaky, drunken hand:

'Lies'

On Monday 28th April 1930 Edith Watts collapsed and died, finally able to join her beloved husband in Hanslope parish church. Was there more to tell? Lies to expose? It's doubtful whether we'll ever know.